A First Family of Tasajara

Bret Harte

Contents

A FIRST FAMILY
OF TASAJARA

BY

Bret Harte

A FIRST FAMILY OF TASAJARA

CHAPTER I

"IT blows, said Joe Wingate.

As if to accent the "words of the speaker a heavy gust of wind at that moment shook the long, light wooden structure which served as the general store of Sidon settlement, in Contra Costa. Even after it had passed a prolonged whistle came through the keyhole, sides, and openings of the closed glass front doors, that served equally for windows, and filled the canvas ceiling which hid the roof above like a bellying wave of enthusiastic emotion seemed to be communicated to a line of straw hats and sou'-westers suspended from a cross beam, and swung them with every appearance of festive rejoicing, while a few dusters, overcoats, and "hickory" shirts hanging on the side walls exhibited such marked though idiotic animation, that it had the effect of a satirical comment on the lazy, purposeless figures of the four living inmates of the store.

Ned Billings momentarily raised his head and shoulders depressed in the back of his wooden arm-chair, glanced wearily around, said, You bet, it's no slouch of a storm," and then lapsed again with further extended legs, and an added sense of comfort.

Here the third figure, which had been leaning listlessly against the shelves, putting aside the arm of a swaying overcoat that seemed to be emptily embracing him, walked slowly from behind the counter to the door, examined its fastenings, and gazed at the prospect. He was the owner of the store and the view was a familiar one. A long stretch of treeless waste before him meeting an equal stretch of dreary sky above, and night hovering somewhere between the two. This was indicated by splashes of darker shadow as if washed in with Indian ink, and a lighter low-lying streak that might have been the horizon, but was not. To the right, on a line with the front door of the store, were several scattered, widely dispersed objects, that, although vague in outline, were rigid enough in angles to suggest sheds or barns, but certainly not trees.

"There's a heap more wet to come afore the wind goes down," he said, glancing at the sky. "Hark to that, now!"

They listened lazily. There was a faint murmur from the shingles above; then suddenly the whole window was filmed and blurred as if the entire prospect had been wiped out with a damp sponge. The man turned listlessly away.

"That's the kind that soaks in; thar won't be much teamin' over Tasajara for the next two weeks, I reckon," said the fourth lounger, who, seated, on a high barrel, was nibbling—albeit critically and fastidiously—biscuits and dried apples alternately from open boxes on the counter. "It's lucky you've got in your winter stock, Harkutt."

The shrewd eyes of Mr. Harkutt, proprietor, glanced at the occupation of the speaker as if even his foresight might have its possible drawbacks, but he said nothing.

"There'll be no show for Sidon until you've got a waggon road from here to the creek," said Billings languidly, from the depths of his chair. "But what's the use o' talkin'? Thar ain't energy enough in all Tasajara to build it. A God-forsaken place, that two months of the year can only be reached by a mail-rider once a week, don't look ez if it was goin' to break its back haulin' in goods and settlers.

I tell ye what, gentlemen,—it makes me sick!" And apparently it had enfeebled him to the extent of interfering with his aim in that expectoration of disgust against the stove with which he concluded his sentence.

"Why don't you build it?" asked Wingate, carelessly.

"I wouldn't on principle," said Billings. "It's Gov'ment work. What did we whoop up things here last spring to elect Kennedy to the Legislation for? What did I rig up my shed and a thousand feet of lumber for benches at the barbicue for? Why, to get Kennedy elected and make him get a Bill passed for the road! That's my share of building it—if it comes to that. And I only wish some folks, that blow enough about what oughter be done to bulge out that ceiling, would only do as much as I have done for Sidon."

As this remark seemed to have a personal as well as local application, the store-keeper diplomatically turned it. "There's a good many as don't believe that a road from here to the creek is going to do any good to Sidon. It's very well to say the creek is an embarcadero, but callin' it so don't put enough water into it to float a steamboat from the bay, nor clear out the reeds and tules in it. Even if the State builds you roads, it ain't got no call to make Tasajara Creek navigable for ye; and as that will cost as much as the road, I don't see where the money's comin' from for both."

"There's water enough in front of 'Lige Curtis' shanty, and his location is only a mile along the bank," returned Billings.

"Water enough for him to laze away his time fishin when he's sober, and deep enough to drown him when he's drunk," said Wingate. "If you call that an embarcadero, you kin buy it any 'Lige,—title, possession, and shanty thrown in, for a demijohn o' whisky."

The fourth man here distastefully threw back a half-nibbled biscuit in the box, and languidly slipped from the barrel to the floor, fastidiously flicking the crumbs from his clothes as he did so. "I reckon somebody'll get it for nothing if 'Lige don't pull up mighty soon. He'll either go on his head with jim-jams or jump into the creek. He's about as near desp'rate as they make 'em, and havin' no partner to look after him, and him alone in the tules, ther's no tellin' what he may do."

Billings, stretched at full length in his chair here gurgled derisively. Desp'rit!—ketch him! Why, that's his little game! He's jist playin' off his desp'rit condition to frighten Sidon. Whenever any one asks him. why he don't go to work, whenever he's hard up for a drink, whenever he's had too much or too little, he's workin' that desp'rit dodge, and even talkin' of killin' himself! Why look here," he continued, momentarily raising himself to a sitting posture in his disgust, "it was only last week he was over at Rawlett's trying to raise provisions and whisky outer his water rights on the creek! Fact, Sir,—had it all written down lawyer-like on paper. Rawlett didn't exactly see it that light, and told him so. Then he up with the desp'rit dodge and began to work that. Said if he had to starve in a swamp like a dog he might as well kill himself at once, and would too if he could afford the weppins. Johnson said it was not a bad idea, and offered to lend him his revolver. Bilson handed up his shotgun, and left it alongside of him, and turned his head away considerate-like and thoughtful, while Rawlett handed him a box of rat pizon over the counter, in case he preferred suthin' more quiet. Well—what did 'Lige do? Nothin'! Smiled kinder sickly, looked sorter wild, and shut up. He didn't suicide much. No, Sir!—He didn't kill himself—not he. Why old Bixby—and he's a Deacon in good standin'—allowed in 'Lige's hearin', and for 'Lige's benefit, that self-destruction was better nor bad example, and proved it by Scripture too. And yet Lige did nothm'! Desp'rit! He's only desp'rit to laze around and fish all day off a log in the tules, and soak up with whisky, until, betwixt fever and ague, and the jumps, he kinder shakes hisself free o' responsibility."

A long silence followed; it was somehow felt that the subject was incongruously exciting; Billings allowed himself to lapse again behind the back of his chair. Meantime it had grown so dark that the dull glow of the stove was beginning to outline a faint halo on the ceiling even while it plunged the further lines of shelves behind the counter into greater obscurity.

"Time to light up, Harkutt—ain't it?" said Wingate tentatively.

"Well, I was reckoning ez it's such a wild night there wouldn't be any use keepin' open, and when you fellows left I'd just shut up for good and make things fast," said Harkutt dubiously. Before his guests had time to fully weigh this delicate hint, another gust of wind shook the tenement and even forced the unbolted upper part of the door to yield far enough to admit an eager current of humid air that seemed to justify the wisdom Harkutt's suggestion. Billings slowly and with a sigh assumed a sitting posture in the chair. The biscuit-nibbler selected a fresh dainty from the counter, and Wingate abstractedly walked to the window and rubbed the glass. Sky and water had already disappeared behind a curtain of darkness that was illuminated. by a single point of light—the lamp in the window of some invisible but nearer house—which threw its rays across the glistening shallows in the road. "Well," said Wingate, buttoning up his coat in slow dejection, "I reckon I oughter be travellin' to help the old woman do the chores before supper." He had just recognized the light in his own dining-room and knew by that sign Midi his long waiting helpmeet; finally done the chores herself.

"Some folks have it mighty easy," said Billings with long-drawn discontent as he struggled to his feet. "You've only a step to go, and yer's me and Peters there—"

indicating the biscuit-nibbler who was beginning to show alarming signs of return-ing to the barrel again—"hev got to trapse five times that distance."

"More'n half a mile, if it comes to that," said Peters gloomily. He paused in put-ting on his overcoat as if thinking better of it, while even the more fortunate and contiguous Wingate languidly lapsed against the counter again.

The moment was a critical one. Billings was evidently also regretfully eyeing the chair he had just quitted. Harkutt resolved on a. heroic effort.

"Come, boys," he said with brisk conviviality, "take a parting drink with me be-fore you go." Producing a black bottle from some obscurity beneath the counter that smelt strongly of india-rubber boots, he placed it with four glasses before his guests. Each made a feint of holding his glass against the opaque window while filling it, although nothing could be seen. A sudden tumult of wind and rain again shook the building, but even after it had passed the glass door still rattled violently.

"Just see what's loose, Peters," said Billings—"you re nearest it."

Peters, still holding the undrained glass in his hand, walked slowly towards it.

"It s suthin'—or somebody outside, he said hesitatingly.

The three others came eagerly to his side. Through the glass, clouded from within by their breath, and filmed from without by the rain, some vague object was moving, and what seemed to be a mop of tangled hair was apparently brushing against the pane. The door shook again, but less strongly. Buildings pressed his face against the glass, "Hol' on," he said in a quick whisper—"it's 'Lige!" But it was too late. Harkutt had already drawn the lower bolt, and a man stumbled from the outer obscurity into the darker room.

The inmates drew away as he leaned back for a moment against the door that closed behind him. Then dimly, but instinctively, discerning the glass of liquor which Wingate still mechanically held in his hand, he reached forward eagerly, took it from Wingate's surprised and unresisting fingers, and drained it at a gulp. The four men laughed vaguely, but not as cheerfully as might.

"I was just shutting up," began Harkutt dubiously

"I won t keep you a minit," said the intruder nervously fumbling in the breast pocket of his hickory shirt. "It's a matter of business—Harkutt—I—" but he was obliged to stop here to wipe his face and forehead with the ends of a loose hand-kerchief tied round his throat. From the action, and what could be seen of his pale, exhausted face, it was evident that the moisture upon it were beads of perspiration, and not the ram which some abnormal heat of his body was converting into vapour from his sodden garments as he stood. there.

"I've got a document here," he began again, producing a roll of paper tremblingly from his pocket, "that I'd like you to glance over, and perhaps youl'd—" his voice, which had been feverishly exalted, here broke and rattled with a cough

Billings, Wingate, and Peters fell apart and looked out of the window. "It's too dark to read anything now, 'Lige," said Harkutt with evasive good humour, "and I ain't lighten' up to-night."

"But I can tell you the substance of it," said. the man. with a faintness that however had all the distinctness of a whisper, "if you'll just step inside a minute. It s a matter of importance and a bargain—"

"I reckon we must be goin'," said Billings to the others with marked emphasis. "We're keepin' Harkutt from shuttin' up." "Goodnight!" "Good-night!" added Peters and Wingate ostentatiously following Billings hurriedly through the door. "So long!

The door closed behind them, leaving Harkutt alone with his importunate intruder. Possibly his resentment at his customers selfish abandonment of him at this moment developed a vague spirit of opposition to them and mitigated his feelings towards 'Lige. He groped his way to the counter, struck a match, and lit a candle. Its feeble rays faintly illuminated the pale, drawn face of the applicant set in a tangle of wet, unkempt, parti-coloured hair. It was not the face of an ordinary drunkard; although tremulous and sensitive from some artificial excitement, there was no engorgement or congestion in the features or complexion, albeit they were morbid and unhealthy. The expression was of a suffering that was as much mental as physical, and yet in some vague way appeared unmeaning—and unheroic.

"I want to see you about selling my place on the creek. I want you to take it on my hands for a bargain. I want to get quit of it, at once, for just enough to take me out o' this. I don't want any profit; only money enough to get away. His utterance, which had a certain kind of cultivation, here grew thick and harsh again, and he looked eagerly at the bottle which stood on the counter.

"Look here, 'Lige," said Harkutt not unkindly. "It's too late to do anythin' to-night. You come in to-morrow." He would have added—"when you're sober," but for a trader s sense of politeness to a possible customer, and probably some doubt of the man's actual condition.

"God knows where or what I may be to-morrow! It would kill me to go back and spend another night as the last, if I don't kill myself on the way to do it."

Harkutt's face darkened grimly. It was indeed as Billings had said! The pitiable weakness of the man's manner not only made his desperation inadequate and ineffective, but even lent it all the cheapness of acting. And, as if to accent his simulation of a part, his fingers feebly groping in his shirt bosom slipped aimlessly and helplessly from the shining handle of a pistol in his pocket to wander hesitatingly towards the bottle on the counter.

Harkutt took the bottle, poured out a glass of the liquor and pushed it before his companion, who drank it eagerly. Whether it gave him more confidence, or his attention was no longer diverted, he went on more collectedly and cheerfully, and with no trace of his previous desperation in his manner. "Come, Harkutt—buy my place. It's a bargain, I tell you. I'll sell it cheap. I only want enough to get away with. Give me twenty-papers the quit-claim—all drawn up and signed." He drew the roll of papers from his pocket again, apparently forgetful of the adjacent weapon.

"Look here, 'Lige," said Harkutt with a business-like straightening of his lips, "I ain't buyin' any land in Tasajara—least of all yours on the creek. I've got more invested here already than I'll ever get back again. But I tell you what I'll do. You say you can't go back to your shanty. Well, seein' how rough it is outside, and that the waters of the creek are probably all over the trail by this time, I reckon you're about right. Now, there s five dollars!" He laid down a coin sharply on the counter. "Take that and go over to Rawlett's and get a bed and some supper. In the mornin' you may be able to strike up a trade with somebody else—or change your mind. How did you get here—on your hoss?"

"Yes."

"He ain't starved yet?"

"No; he can eat grass—I can't."

Either the liquor or Harkutt's practical, unsentimental treatment of the situation seemed to give him confidence. He met Harkutt's eye more steadily as the latter went on, "You kin turn your hoss for the night into my stock corral next to Rawlett's. It'll save you payin' for fodder and stablin'."

The man took up the coin with a certain slow gravity which was almost like dignity. "Thank you," he said, laying the paper on the counter. "I'll leave that as security."

"Don't want it, 'Lige," said Harkutt pushing it back.

"I'd rather leave it."

"But suppose you have a chance to sell it to somebody at Rawlett's?" continued Harkutt with a precaution that seemed ironical.

"I don't think there's much chance of that."

He remained quiet looking at Harkutt with an odd expression as he rubbed the edge of the coin that he held between his fingers abstractedly on the counter. Something in his gaze—rather perhaps the apparent absence of anything in it approximate to the present occasion—was beginning to affect Harkutt with a vague uneasiness. Providentially a resumed onslaught of wind and rain against the panes effected a diversion. "Come," he said with brisk practicality, "you'd better hurry on to Rawlett's before it gets worse. Have your clothes dried by his fire, take suthin' to eat, and you'll be all right." He rubbed his hands cheerfully, as if summarily disposing of the situation, and incidentally of all 'Lige's troubles, and walked with him to the door. Nevertheless as the man s look remained unchanged, he hesitated a moment with his hand on the handle, in the hope that he would say something, even if only to repeat his appeal, but he did not. Then Harkutt opened the door; the man moved mechanically out, and at the distance of a few feet seemed to melt into the rain and darkness. Harkutt remained for a moment with his face pressed against the glass. After an interval he thought he heard the faint splash of hoofs in the shallows of the road; he opened the door softly and looked out.

The light had disappeared from the nearest house; only an uncertain bulk of shapeless shadows remained. Other remoter and more vague outlines nearer the horizon seemed to have a funereal suggestion of tombs and grave mounds and one—a low shed near the road—looked not unlike a halted bier. He hurriedly put up the shutters in a momentary lulling of the wind, and re-entering the store began to fasten them from within.

While thus engaged an inner door behind the counter opened softly and cautiously, projecting a brighter light into the deserted apartment from some sacred domestic interior with the warm and wholesome incense of cooking. It served to introduce also the equally agreeable presence of a young girl who, after assuring herself of the absence of every one but the proprietor, idly slipped into the store, and placing her rounded elbows, from which her sleeves were uprolled, upon the counter, leaned lazily upon them with both hands supporting her dimpled chin and gazed indolently at him. So indolently that with her pretty face once fixed in this comfortable attitude she was constrained to follow his movements with her eyes alone, and often at an uncomfortable angle. It was evident that she offered the final but charming illustration of the enfeebling listlessness of Sidon.

"So those loafers have gone at last," she said meditatively. "They'll take root here some day, pop. The idea of three strong men like that lazing round for two mortal hours mortal hours doin' nothin'. Well!" As if too emphasize her disgust she threw her whole weight upon the counter by swinging her feet from the floor to touch the' shelves behind her.

Mr. Harkutt only replied by a slight grunt as he continued to screw on the shutters.

"Want me to help you, dad?" she said without moving.

Mr. Harkutt muttered something unintelligible which, however, seemed to imply a negative, and her attention here feebly wandered to the roll of papers, and she began slowly and lazily to read it aloud.

" 'For value received, I hereby sell, assign, and transfer to Daniel D. Harkutt all my right, title and interest in, and to the undivided half of, Quarter Section 4, Range 5, Tasajara Township'—hum—hum," she murmured, running her eyes to the bottom of the page. "Why, Lord! It's that 'Lige Curtis!" she laughed. "The idea of him having property ! Why, dad, you ain't been that silly!"

"Put down that paper, miss," he said aggrievedly; "bring the candle here, and help me to find one of these infernal screws that s dropped.

The girl indolently disengaged herself from the counter and Elijah Curtis's transfer, and brought the candle to her father. The screw was presently found and the last fastening secured. ."Supper gettin' cold, dad," she said with a slight yawn. Her father sympathetically responded by stretching himself from his stooping position, and the two passed through the private door into inner domesticity, leaving the already forgotten paper lying with other articles of barter on the counter.

CHAPTER II

WITH the closing of the little door behind them they seemed to have shut out the turmoil and vibration of the storm. The reason became apparent when after a few paces they descended half-a-dozen steps to a lower landing. This disclosed the fact that the dwelling part of the Sidon General Store was quite below the level of the shop and the road, and on the slope of the solitary undulation of the Tasajara plain—a little ravine that fell away to a brawling stream below. The only arboreous growth of Tasajara clothed its banks in the shape of willows and alders that set compactly around the quaint, irregular dwelling which straggled down the ravine and looked upon a slope of bracken and foliage on either side. The transition from the black, treeless, storm-swept plain to this sheltered declivity, was striking and suggestive. From the opposite bank one might fancy that the youthful and original dwelling had ambitiously mounted the crest, but appalled at the dreary prospect beyond, had gone no further; while from the road it seemed as if the fastidious proprietor had tried to draw a line between the vulgar trading-post, with which he was obliged to face the coarser civilization of too place, and. the privacy of his domestic life. The real fact, however, was, that the ravine furnished wood and water; and as Nature also provided one wall of the house—as in the well-known example of aboriginal cave dwellings,—commended itself to Sidon on the ground of involving little labour.

Howbeit, from the two open windows of the sitting-room which they had entered only the faint pattering of dripping boughs, and a slight murmur from the swollen brook, indicated the storm that shook the upper plain, and the cool breath of laurel, syringa, and alder was wafted through the neat apartment. Passing through that pleasant rural atmosphere they entered the kitchen, a much larger room, which, appeared to serve occasionally as a dining-room and where supper was already laid out. A stout, comfortable looking woman—who had, however, a singularly permanent expression of pained sympathy upon her face—welcomed them in tones of gentle commiseration.

"Ah, there you be, you two! Now sit ye right down, dears! do. You must be tired out; and you, Phemie, love, draw up by your poor father. There—that's right. You'll be better soon."

"There was certainly no visible sign of suffering or exhaustion on the part of either father or daughter, nor the slightest apparent earthly reason why they should be expected to exhibit any. But, as already intimated, it was part of Mrs. Harkutt's generous idiosyncracy to look upon all humanity as suffering and toiling; to be petted, humoured, consoled with, and fed. It had, in the course of years, imparted a singularly caressing sadness to her voice, and given her the habit of ending her sentences with a melancholy cooing and an unintelligible murmur of agreement. It was undoubtedly sincere and sympathetic, but at times inappropriate and distressing. It had lost her the friendship of the one humorist of Tasajara, whose best jokes she had received with such heartfelt commiseration, and such pained appreciation of the evident labour involved, as to reduce him to silence.

Accustomed as Mr. Harkutt was to his wife's peculiarity, he was not above assuming a certain slightly fatigued attitude befitting it. "Yes," he said, with a vague sigh, "where's Clemmie?"

"Lyin' down since dinner; she reckoned she wouldn't get up to supper, she returned soothingly. "Phemie's goin' to take her up some sass and tea. The poor dear child wants a change."

"She wants to go to 'Frisco, and so do I, pop," said Phemie, leaning her elbow half over her father's plate. "Come, pop, say do—just for a week."

"Only for a week," murmured the commiserating Mrs. Harkutt.

"Perphaps," responded Harkutt, with gloomy sarcasm, "ye wouldn't mind tellin' me how you're goin' to get there, and where the money's comin' from to take you? There's no teamin' over Tasajara till the rain stops, and no money comin in till the ranchmen can move their stun. There ain't a hundred dollars in all Tasajara— at least there am t been the first red cent of it paid across my counter for a fortint! Perhaps if you do go, you wouldn't mind takin' me and the store along with ye, and leavin' us there."

"Yes, dear," said Mrs. Harkutt, with sympathetic but shameless tergiversation. "Don't bother your poor father, Phemie, love, don't you see he's just tired out? And you're not eatin' anything, dad."

As Mr. Harkutt was uneasily conscious that he had been eating heartily in spite of his financial difficulties he turned the subject abruptly. "Where's John Milton?"

Mrs. Harkutt shaded her eyes with her hand, and gazed meditatively on the floor before the fire and in the chimney corner for her only son, baptised under that historic title. "He was here a minit ago," she said doubtfully. "I really can t think where he s gone. But," as-suringly, "it ain't far."

"He's skipped with one o' those story books he's borrowed," said Phemie. "He's always doin' it. Like as not he's reading with a candle in the wood-shed. We'll all be burnt up some night."

"But he's got through his chores," interposed Mrs. Harkutt deprecatingly.

"Yes," continued Harkutt aggrievedly, "but instead of goin' to bed, or adding up bills, or takin count o' stock, or even doin' sums or suthin' useful, he's ruinin' his eyes and wastin' his time over trash." He rose and walked slowly into the sitting-room, followed by his daughter and a murmur of commiseration from his wife. .But Mrs. Harkutt's ministration for the present did not pass beyond her domain—the kitchen.

"I reckon ye ain't expectin' anybody to-night, Phemie?" said Mr. Harkutt, sinking into a chair and placing his slippered feet against the wall.

"No," said Phemie, "unless something possesses that sappy .little Parmlee to make one of his visitations. John Milton says that out on the road it blows so you can't stand up. It's just like that idiot Parmlee to be blown in here, and not have strength of mind enough to get away again."

Mr. Harkutt smiled. It was that arch yet approving, severe yet satisfied smile with which the deceived male parent usually receives any depreciation of the ordinary young man by his daughters. Euphemia was no giddy thing be carried away by young men's attentions—not she! Sitting back comfortably in his rocking –chair he said, "Play something."

The young girl went to the closet and took from the top shelf an excessively ornamented accordion—the opulent gift of a reckless admirer. It was so inordinately decorated, so gorgeous in the blaze of papier maché, mother-of pearl, and tortoiseshell on keys and keyboard, and so ostentatiously radiant in the pink silk of its bellows, that it seemed to overawe the plainly furnished room with its splendours "You ought to keep it on the table in a glass vase, Phemie," said her father admiringly.

"And have him think I worshipped it!—not me, indeed! He's conceited enough already," she returned saucily.

Mr. Harkutt again smiled his approbation, then deliberately closed his eyes and threw his head back in comfortable anticipation of the coming strains.

It is to be regretted that in brilliancy, finish, and even cheerfulness of quality they were not up to the suggestions of the keys and keyboard. The most discreet and cautious effort on the part of the young performer seemed only to produce startlingly unexpected, but instantly suppressed complaints from the instrument, accompanied by impatient interjections of "no, no," from the girl herself. Nevertheless, with her pretty eyebrows knitted in some charming distress of memory, her little mouth half open between an apologetic smile and the exertion of working the bellows, with her white, rounded arms partly lifted up and waving before her, she was pleasantly distracting to the eye. Gradually, as the scattered strains were marshalled into something like an air, she began to sing also, glossing over the instrumental weaknesses, filling in certain dropped notes and omissions, and otherwise assisting the ineffectual accordion with a youthful but not unmusical voice. The song was a lugubrious, religious chant; under its influence the house seemed to sink into greater quiet, permitting in the intervals the murmur of the swollen creek to appear more distinct, and even the far moaning of the wind on the plain to become faintly audible. At last, having fairly mastered the instrument, Phemie got into the full swing of the chant. Unconstrained by any criticism, carried away by the sound of her own voice, and perhaps a youthful love for mere uproar, or possibly desirous to drown her father's voice, which had unexpectedly joined with a discomposing bass their conjoined utterances seemed to threaten the frail structure of their dwelling, even as the gale had distended the store behind them. When they ceased at last it was in an accession of dripping from the apparently stirred leaves outside. And then a voice, evidently from the moist depths of the abyss below, called out,

"Hullo, there!"

Phemie put down the accordion, said, "Who's that now?" went to the window, lazily leaned her elbows on the sill and peered into the darkness. Nothing was to be seen; the open space of dimly outlined landscape had that blank, uncommunicative impenetrability with which Nature always confronts and surprises us at such moments. It seemed to Phemie that she was the only human being present. Yet after the feeling had passed she fancied she heard the wash of the current against some object in the stream, half stationary and half resisting.

"Is any one down there? Is that you, Mr. Parmlee?" she called.

There was a pause. Some invisible auditor said to another, "It's a young lady." Then the first voice rose again in a more deferential tone. Are we anywhere near Sidon?"

"This is Sidon," answered Harkutt, who had risen and was now quite obliterating his daughter's outline at the window.

"Thank you," said the voice. "Can we land anywhere here—on this bank?"

"Run down, pop, they're strangers," said the girl with excited, almost childish eagerness.

"Hold. on," called out Harkutt, "I'll be thar in a moment!" He hastily thrust his feet into a pair of huge boots, clapped on an oilskin hat and waterproof, and disappeared through a door that led to a lower staircase. Phemie still at the window—albeit with a newly added sense of self-consciousness—hung out breathlessly. Presently a beam of light from the lower depths of the house shot out into the darkness. It was her father with a bull's-eye lantern. As he held it up and clambered cautiously down the bank, its rays fell upon the turbid rushing stream, and what appeared to be a rough raft of logs held with difficulty against the bank by two men with long poles. In its centre was a roll of blankets, a valise and saddle-bags, and the shining brasses of some odd-looking instruments.

As Mr. Harkutt, supporting himself by a willow branch that overhung the current, held up the lantern, the two men rapidly transferred their freight from the raft to the bank, and leaped ashore. The action gave an impulse to the raft which, no longer held in position by the poles, swung broadside to the current and was instantly swept into the darkness.

Not a word had been spoken, but now the voices of the men rose freely together. Phemie listened with intense expectation. The explanation was simple. They were surveyors who had been caught by the overflow on Tasajara plain, had abandoned their horses on the bank of Tasajara Creek, and with a hastily constructed raft had entrusted themselves and their instruments to the current. "But, said Harkutt quickly, "there's no connection between Tasajara Creek and this stream."

The two men laughed. "There is now," said one of them.

"But Tasajara Creek is a part of the bay," said the astonished Harkutt, "and this stream rises inland and only runs into the bay four miles lower down. And I don't see how—"

"You are almost twelve feet lower here than Tasajara Creek," said the first man with a certain professional authority, "and that's why. There's more water than Tasajara Creek can carry and it's seeking the bay this way. Look, he continued, taking the lantern from Harkutt's hand and casting its rays on the stream, "that's salt drift from the upper bay, and part of Tasajara Creek's running by your house now! Don't be alarmed," he added reassuringly, glancing at the staring storekeeper. "You're all right here; this is only the overflow find will find its level soon."

But Mr. Harkutt remained gazing abstractedly at the smiling speaker. From the window above the impatient Phemie was wondering why he kept the strangers waiting in the rain while he talked about things that were perfectly plain. It was so like a man!

"Then there's a waterway straight to Tasajara Creek," he said slowly.

"There is, as long as this flood lasts," returned the first speaker promptly; and a cutting through the bank of two or three hundred yards would make it permanent. Well, what's the matter with that?"

"Nothin'," said Harkutt hurriedly. "I am only considering! But come in, dry yourselves, and take suthin'."

The light over the rushing water was withdrawn .and the whole prospect sank back into profound darkness. Mr. Harkutt had disappeared with his guests. Then there was the familiar shuffle of his feet on the staircase, followed by other more cautious footsteps that grew delicately and even courteously deliberate as they approached. At which the young girl in some new sense of decorum drew in her pretty head, glanced around the room quickly, reset the tidy on her father's chair, placed the resplendent accordion like an ornament in the exact centre of the table, and then vanished into the hall as Mr. Harkutt entered with the strangers.

They were both of the same age and appearance, but the principal speaker was evidently the superior of his companion, and although their attitude to each other was equal and familiar, it could be easily seen that he was the leader. .He had a smooth, beardless face, with a critical expression of eye and mouth that might have been fastidious and supercilious but for the kindly, humorous perception that tempered it. His quick eye swept the apartment and then fixed itself upon the accordion, but a smile lit up his face as he said quietly,

"I hope we haven't frightened the musician away. It was bad enough to have interrupted the young lady."

"No, no," said Mr. Harkutt, who seemed to have lost his abstraction in the nervousness of hospitality. "I reckon she's only lookin' after her sick sister. But come into the kitchen, both of you, straight off, and while you're dryin' your clothes, mother'll fix you suthin' hot."

"We only need to change our boots and stockings, we've some dry ones in our pack down stairs," said the first speaker hesitatingly.

"I'll fetch' 'em up and you can change in the kitchen. The old woman won't mind," said Harkutt reassuringly. "Come along." He led the way to the kitchen, the two strangers exchanged a glance of humorous perplexity and followed.

The quiet of the little room was once more unbroken. A far-off commiserating murmur indicated that Mrs. Harkutt was receiving her guests. The cool breath of the wet leaves without slightly disturbed the white dimity curtains, and somewhere from the darkened eaves there was a still, somnolent drip. Presently a hurried whisper and. a half laugh appeared to be suppressed in the outer passage or hall. There was another moment of hesitation and the door opened suddenly and ostentatioulsly, disclosing Phemie with a taller and slighter young woman, her elder sister, at her side. Perceiving that the room was empty they both said "Oh!" yet with a certain artificiality of manner that was evidently a lingering trace of some previous formal attitude they had assumed. Then without further speech they each selected a chair and a position, having first shaken out their dresses, and gazed silently at each other.

It may be said briefly that sitting thus—in spite of their unnatural attitude, or perhaps rather because of its suggestion of a photographic pose—they made a striking picture and accented their separate peculiarities. They were both pretty, but the taller girl, apparently the elder, had an ideal refinement and regularity of feature which was not only unlike Phemie, but gratuitously unlike the rest of her family, and as hopelessly and even wantonly inconsistent with her surroundings as was the elaborately ornamented accordion on the centre table. She was one of those occasional creatures, episodical in the South and West, who might have been stamped

with some vague ante-natal impression of a mother given to over-sentimental contemplation of Books of Beauty and Albums rather than the family matures; offspring
of typical men and women, and yet themselves incongruous to any known local or
even general type. The long swan-like neck, tendrilled hair, swimming eyes, and
small patrician head, had never lived or moved before in Tasajara or the West,
nor perhaps even existed except as a personified "Constancy," "Meditation," or the
"Baron's Bride" in mezzotint or copper-plate. Even the girl's common pink print
dress with its high sleeves and shoulders could not conventionalize these original
outlines; and the hand that rested stiffly on the back of her chair, albeit neither over
white nor well-kept, looked as if it had never held anything but a lyre, a rose, or a
good book. Even the few sprays of wild jessamine which she had placed in the coils
of her waving hair, although a local fashion, became her as a special ornament.

The two girls kept their constrained and artificially elaborated attitude for a few
moments, accompanied by the murmur of voices in. the kitchen, the monotonous
drip of the eaves before the window, and the far-off sough of the wind. Then Phemie suddenly broke into a constrained giggle, which she however quickly smoth-
ered as she had the accordion, and with the same look of mischievous distress.

"I'm astonished at you, Phemie," said Clementina in a deep contralto voice,
which seemed even deeper from its restraint. "You don't seem to have any sense.
Anybody'l'd think you'd never had seen a stranger before."

"Saw him before you did, retorted Phemie pertly. But here a pushing of chairs
and shuffling of feet in the kitchen checked her. Clementina fixed an abstracted
gaze on the ceiling; Phemie regarded a leaf on the window sill with photographic
rigidity as the door opened to the strangers and her father.

The look of undisguised satisfaction which lit the young men's faces relieved
Mr. Harkutt's awkward introduction of any embarrassment, and almost before Phemie was fully aware of it, she found herself talking rapidly and in a high key with
Mr. .Lawrence Grant, the surveyor, while her sister was equally, although more
sedately, occupied with Mr. Stephen Rice, his assistant. But the enthusiasm of the
strangers, and the desire to please and be pleased, was so genuine and contagious
that presently the accordion was brought into requisition, and Mr. Grant exhibited
a surprising faculty of accompaniment to Mr. Rice's tenor, in which both the girls
joined.

Then a game of cards with partners followed, into which the rival parties introduced such delightful and shameless obviousness of cheating, and displayed such fascinating and exaggerated partisanship that the game resolved itself into a hilarious mêlée, to which peace was restored only by an exhibition of tricks of legerdemain with the cards by the young surveyor. All of which Mr. Harkutt supervised patronizingly with occasional fits of abstraction, from his rocking-chair; and later Mrs. Harkutt from her kitchen threshold, wiping her arms on her apron and commiseratingly observing that she "declared the young folks looked better already."

But it was here a more dangerous element of mystery and suggestion was added by Mr. Lawrence Grant in the telling of Miss. Euphemia's fortune from the cards before nun, and. that young lady, pink with excitement, fluttered her little hands not unlike timid birds over the cards to be drawn, taking them from him with an audible twitter of anxiety and great doubts whether a certain "fair-haired gentleman" was in. hearts or diamonds.

"Here are two strangers," said Mr. Grant with extraordinary gravity laying down the carets, and here is a 'journey,' this is 'unexpected news,' and this ten of diamonds means 'great wealth' to you, which you see follows the advent of the two strangers and. is some way connected with them."

"Oh, indeed," said the young lady with great pertness and a toss of her head. "I suppose they've got the money with them."

"No, though it reaches you through them," he replied with unflinching solemnity "Wait a bit, I have it! I see, I've made a mistake with this card. It signifies a journey or a road. Queer! Isn't it, Steeve? It' the road."

"It is queer," said Rice with equal gravity; "but it's so. The road, sure!" Nevertheless he looked up into the large eyes of Clementina with a certain confidential air of truthfulness.

"You see, ladies," continued the surveyor appealing to them with unabashed rigidity of feature, the cards don't lie! Luckily we are in a position to corroborate them. The road in question is a secret known only to us and some capitalists in San Francisco. In fact even they don't know that it is feasible until we report to them. But I don't mind telling you now, as a slight return for your charming hospitality, that the road is a railroad from Oakland to Tasajara Creek of which we've just made the preliminary survey. So you see what the cards mean is this: You're not far from Tasajara Creek; in fact with a very little expense your father could connect this stream with the creek, and have a waterway straight to the railroad terminus. That's the wealth the cards promise; and if your father knows how to take a hint he can make his fortune!"

It was impossible to say which was the most dominant in the face of the speaker, the expression of assumed gravity or the twinkling of humour in his eyes. The two girls with superior feminine perception divined that there was much truth in what he said, albeit they didn't entirely understand it, and what they did understand— except the man's good-humoured motive—was not particularly interesting. In fact they were slightly disappointed. What had promised to be an audaciously flirtatious declaration, and even a mischievous suggestion of marriage, had resolved itself into something absurdly practical and business-Like.

No so Mr. Harkutt. He quickly rose from his chair, and leaning over the table, with his eyes fixed on the card as if it really signified the rail road, repeated quickly: "Railroad, eh! What's that? A railroad to Tasajara Creek? Ye don't mean it!—That is—it ain't a sure thing?"

"Perfectly sure. The money is ready in San Francisco now, and by this time next year—"

"A railroad to Tasajara Creek!" continued Harkutt hurriedly. "What part of it? Where?"

"At the embarcadero naturally," responded Grant. "There isn't but the one place for the terminus. There's an old shanty there now—belongs to somebody."

"Why, pop!" said Phemie with sudden recollection, "ain't it 'Lige Curtis's house? The land he offered—"

"Hush!" said her father.

"You know the one written in that bit of paper," continued the innocent Phemie.

"Hush! will you? God A'mighty! are you goin' to mind me? Are you goin' to keep up your jabber when I'm speakin' to the gentlemen? Is that your manners? What next, I wonder!"

The sudden and unexpected passion of the speaker, the incomprehensible change in his voice, and the utterly disproportionate exaggeration of his attitude towards his daughters, enforced an instantaneous silence. The rain began to drip audibly at the window, the rush of the river sounded distinctly from without, even the shaking of the front part of the dwelling by the distant gale became perceptible. An angry flash sprang for an instant to the young assistant's eye, but it met the cautious glance of his friend, and together both discreetly sought the table. The two girls alone remained white and collected. "Will you go on with my fortune, Mr. Grant?" said Phemie quietly.

A certain respect, perhaps not before observable, was suggested in the surveyor's tone as he smilingly replied, "Certainly, I was only waiting for you to show your confidence in me," and took up the cards.

"Mr. Harkutt coughed. "It looks as if that blamed wind had blown suthin' loose in the store," he said affectedly. "I reckon I'll go and see." He hesitated a moment and then disappeared in the passage. Yet even here he stood irresolute, looking at the closed door behind him, and passing his hand over his still flushed face. Presently he slowly and abstractedly ascended the flight of steps, entered the smaller passage that led to the back door of the shop and opened it.

He was at first a little startled at the halo of light from the still glowing stove which the greater obscurity of the long room had heightened rather than diminished. Then he passed behind the counter, but here the box of biscuits which occupied the centre and cast a shadow over it, compelled him to grope vaguely for what he sought. Then he stopped suddenly, the paper he had just found dropping from his fingers, and said sharply:

"Who's there?"

"Me, pop."

"John Milton?"

"Yes, sir."

"What the devil are you doin' there, sir?"

"Readin'."

It was true. The boy was half reclining in a most distorted posture on two chairs, his figure in deep shadow, but his book was raised above his head so as to catch the red glow of the stove on the printed page. Even then his father's angry interruption scarcely diverted his preoccupation; he raised himself in his chair mechanically with his eyes still fixed on his book. Seeing which his father quickly regained the paper, but continued his objurgation.

"How dare you? Clear off to bed, will you! Do you hear me? Pretty goings on," he added as if to justify his indignation. "Sneakin' in here—and lyin' 'round at this time o' night! Why, if I hadn't come in here to—"

"What?" asked the boy mechanically, catching vaguely at the unfinished sentence and staring automatically at the paper in his father's hand.

"Nothin', sir! Go to bed, I tell you! Will you? What are you standin' gawpin' at?" continued Harkutt furiously.

The boy regained his feet slowly and passed his father, but not without noticing with the same listless yet ineffaceable perception of child-hood that he was hurriedly concealing the paper in his pocket. With the same youthful inconsequence, wondering at this more than at the interruption, which was no novel event, he went slowly out of the room.

Harkutt listened to the retreating tread of his bare feet in the passage and then carefully locked the door. Taking the paper from his pocket, and borrowing the idea he had just objurgated in his son, he turned it towards the dull glow of the stove and attempted to read it. But perhaps lacking the patience as well as the keener sight of youth, he was forced to relight the candle which he had left on the counter, and reperused the paper. Yes! there was certainly no mistake! Here was the actual description of the property which the surveyor had just indicated as the future terminus of the new railroad, and here it was conveyed to him—Daniel Harkutt! What was that? Somebody knocking! What did this continual interruption mean? An odd superstitious fear now mingled with his irritation.

The sound appeared to come from the front shutters. It suddenly occurred to him that the light might be visible through the crevices. He hurriedly extinguished it, and went to the door.

"Who's there?"

"Me—Peters. Want to speak to you."

"Mr. Harkutt with evident reluctance drew the bolts. The wind, still boisterous and besieging, did the rest, and precipitately propelled Peters through the carefully guarded opening. But his surprise at finding himself in the darkness seemed to forestall any explanation of his visit.

"Well," he said with an odd mingling of reproach and suspicion. "I declare I saw a light here just this minit! That's queer."

"Yes, I put it out just now. I was goin' away," replied Harkutt, with ill-disguised impatience.

"What! been here ever since?"

"No," said Harkutt curtly.

"Well, I want to speak to ye about 'Lige. Seein' the candle shinin' through the chinks I thought he might be still with ye. If he ain't, it looks bad. Light up, can't ye! I want to show you something."

There was a peremptoriness in his tone that struck Harkutt disagreeably, but observing that he was carrying something in his hand, he somewhat nervously re-lit the candle and faced him. Peters had a hat in his hand. It was 'Lige's!

"'Bout an hour after we fellers left here," said Peters, "I heard the rattlin' of hoofs on the road, and then it seemed to stop just by my house. I went out with a lantern, and, darn my skin! if there warn't 'Lige's hoss, the saddle empty, and 'Lige nowhere! I looked round and called him—but nothing were to be seen. Thinkin' he might have slipped off—tho' ez a general rule drunken men don't, and he is a good rider—I followed down the road, lookin' for him. I kept on follerin' it down to your run, half a mile below."

"But," began Harkutt, with a quick nervous laugh, "you don't reckon that because that he—"

"Hold on!" said Peters, grimly producing a revolver from his side pocket with the stock and barrel clogged and streaked with mud. "I found that, too—and look! one barrel discharged! And," he added hurriedly, as approaching a climax, "look ye—what I nat'rally took for wet from the rain—inside that hat—was—blood!"

"Nonsense!" said Harkutt, putting the hat aside with a new fastidiousness. "You don't think—"

"I think," said Peters, lowering his voice, "I think, by God! he's bin and done it!"

"No!"

"Sure! Oh, it's all very well for Billings and the rest of that conceited crowd to sneer and sling their ideas of 'Lige gen'rally as they did jess now here—but I'd like 'em to see that." It was difficult to tell if Mr. Peters's triumphant delight in confuting his late companions' theories had not even usurped in his mind the importance of the news he brought as it had of any human sympathy with it.

"Look here," returned Harkutt earnestly, yet with a singularly cleared brow and a more natural manner. "You ought to take them things over to Squire Kerby's, right off, show 'em to him. You kin tell him how you left 'Lige here, and say that I can prove by my daughter that he went away about ten minutes after—at least, not more than fifteen." Like all unprofessional humanity, Mr. Harkutt had an exaggerated conception of the majesty of unimportant detail in the eye of the law. "I'd go with you myself," he added quickly, "but I've got company strangers here."

"How did he look when he left—kinder wild?" suggested Peters.

Harkutt had begun to feel the prudence of present reticence. "Well," he said, cautiously, "you saw how he looked."

"You wasn't rough with him?—that might have sent him off, you know," said Peters.

"No," said Harkutt, forgetting himself in a quick indignation, "no, I not only treated him to another drink, but gave him—" he stopped suddenly and awkwardly.

"Eh?" said Peters.

"Some good advice—you know," said Harkutt hastily. "But come, you'l'd better hurry over to the squire's. You know you've made the discovery; your evidence is important, and there's a law that obliges you to give information at once."

The excitement of discovery, and the triumph over his disputants, being spent, Peters, after the Sidon fashion, evidently did not relish activity as a duty. "You know," he said dubiously, "he mightn't be dead, after all."

Harkutt became a trifle distant. "You know your own opinion of the thing," he replied after a pause. "You've circumstantial evidence enough to see the squire, and set others to work on it; and," he added significantly, "you've done your share then, and can wipe your hands of it, eh?"

"That's so," said Peters eagerly. "I'll just run over to the squire."

"And on account of the women folks, you know, and the strangers here, I'll say nothin' about it to-night,' added Harkutt.

Peters nodded his head, and taking up the hat of the unfortunate Elijah with a certain hesitation as if he feared it had already lost its dramatic intensity as a witness, disappeared into the storm and darkness again. A lurking gust of wind lying in ambush somewhere seemed to swoop down on him as if to prevent further indecision and whirl him away in the direction of the justice's house; and Mr. Harkutt shut the door, bolted it, and walked aimlessly back to the counter.

From a slow, deliberate and cautious man, he seemed to have changed within an hour to an irresolute and capricious one. He took the paper from his pocket and, unlocking the money drawer of his counter, folded into a small compass that which now seemed to be the last testament of Elijah Curtis, and placed it in a recess. Then he went to the back door and paused, then returned, reopened the money drawer, took out the paper and again buttoned it in his hip pocket, standing by the stove and staring abstractedly at the dull glow of the fire. He even went through the mechanical process of raking down the ashes—solely to gain time and as an excuse for delaying some other necessary action.

He was thinking what he should do. Had the question of his right to retain and make use of that paper been squarely offered to him an hour ago, he would have, without doubt, decided that he ought not to keep it. Even now, looking at it as an abstract principle, he did not deceive himself in the least. But Nature has the reprehensible habit of not presenting these questions to us squarely and fairly, and it is remarkable that in most of our offending the abstract principle is never the direct issue. Mr. Harkutt was conscious of having been unwillingly led step by step into a difficult, not to say dishonest, situation-and against his own seeking. He had never asked Elijah to sell him the property; he had distinctly declined it; it had even been forced upon him as security for the pittance he so freely gave him. This proved (to himself) that he himself was honest; it was only the circumstances that were queer. Of course if Elijah had lived he, Harkutt, might have tried to drive some bargain with him before the news of the railroad survey came out—for that was only business. But Elijah was dead, who would be a penny the worse or better but himself if he chose to consider the whole thing as a lucky speculation, and his gift of five dollars as the price he paid for it? Nobody could think that he had calculated upon 'Lige's suicide, any more than that the property would become valuable. In fact if it came to that, if 'Lige had really contemplated killing himself as a hopeless bankrupt after taking Harkutt's money as a loan, it was a swindle on his—Harkutt's—good-nature. He worked himself into a rage, which he felt was innately virtuous, at this tyranny of cold principle over his own warm-hearted instincts, but if it came to the law, he'd stand by law and not sentiment. He'd just let them—by which he vaguely meant the world, Tasajara, and. possibly his own conscience—see that no wasn't a sentimental fool, and he'd freeze on to that paper and that property!

Only he ought to have spoken out before. He ought to have told the surveyor at once that he owned the land. He ought to have said: Why, that's my land. I bought it of that drunken 'Lige Curtis for a song and out of charity." Yes, that was the only real trouble, and that came from his own goodness, his own extravagant sense of justice and right—his own cursed good-nature. Yet, on second thoughts, he didn't know why he was obliged to tell the surveyor. Time enough when the company wanted to buy the land. As soon as it was settled that 'Lige was dead he'd openly claim the property. But what if he wasn't dead? or they couldn't find his body? or he had only disappeared? His plain, matter-of fact face contracted and darkened. Of course he couldn't ask the company to wait for him to settle that point. He had the power to dispose of the property under that paper, and—he should do it. If 'Lige turned up that was another matter, and he and 'Lige could arrange it between them. He was quite firm here, and oddly enough quite relieved in getting rid of what appeared only a simple question of detail. He never suspected that he was contemplating the one irretrievable step, and summarily dismissing the whole ethical question.

He turned away from the stove, opened the back door, and walked with a more determined step through the passage to the sitting-room. But here he halted again on the threshold with a quick return of his old habits of caution. The door was slightly open; apparently his angry outbreak of an hour ago had not affected the spirits of his daughters, for he could hear their hilarious voices mingling with those of the strangers. They were evidently still fortune-telling, but this time it was the prophetic and divining accents of Mr. Rice addressed to Clementina which were' now plainly audible.

"I see heaps of money and a great many friends in the change that is coming to you. Dear me! how many suitors! But I cannot promise you any marriage as brilliant as my friend has just offered your sister. You may be certain, however, that you'll have your own choice in this, as you have in all things."

"Thank you for nothing," said Clementina's voice. "But what are those horrid black cards beside them?—that's trouble, I' m sure."

"Not for you, though near you. Perhaps some one you don't care much for and don't understand will have a heap of trouble on your account—yes, on account of these very riches; see, he follows the ten of diamonds. It may be a suitor—it may be some one now in the house perhaps."

"He means himself, Miss Clementina," struck in Grant's voice laughingly.

"You're not listening, Miss Harkutt," said Rice with half serious reproach. "Perhaps you know who it is?"

But Miss Clementina's reply was simply a hurried recognition of her fathers pale face that here suddenly confronted her with the opening door.

"Why, it's Father!"

CHAPTER III

IN his strange mental condition even the change from Harkutt's feeble candle to the outer darkness for a moment blinded Elijah Curtis, yet it was part of that mental condition that he kept moving steadily forward as in a trance or dream, though at first purposelessly. Then it occurred to him that he was really looking for his horse, and that the animal was not there. This for a moment confused and frightened him, first with the supposition that he had not brought him at all, but that it was part of his delusion; secondly, with the conviction that without his horse he could neither proceed on the course suggested by Harkutt, nor take another more vague one that was dimly in his mind. Yet in his hopeless vacillation it seemed a relief that now neither was practicable, and that he need do nothing. Perhaps it was a mysterious Providence!

The explanation, however, was much simpler. The horse had been taken by the luxurious and indolent Billings unknown to his companions. Overcome at the dreadful prospect of walking home in that weather, this perfect product of lethargic Sidon had artfully allowed Peters and Wingate to precede him, and, cautiously unloosing the tethered animal, had safely passed them in the darkness. When he gained his own enclosure he had lazily dismounted, and, with a sharp cut on the mustang s haunches, sent him galloping back to rejoin his master, with what result has been already told by the unsuspecting .Peters in this preceding chapter.

Yet no conception of this possibility entered Lige Curtis s alcoholized consciousness, part of whose morbid phantasy it was to distort or exaggerate all natural phenomena. He had a vague idea that he could not go back to Harkutt's; already his visit seemed to have happened long, long ago, and could not be repeated. He would walk on, enwrapped in this uncompromising darkness which concealed everything, suggested everything, and was responsible for everything.

It was very dark, for the wind, having lulled, no longer thinned the veil of clouds above, nor dissipated a steaming mist that appeared to rise from the sodden plain. Yet he moved easily through the darkness, seeming to be upheld by it as something tangible, upon which he might lean. At times he thought he heard voices—not a particular voice he was thinking of, but strange voices—of course unreal to his present fancy. And then he heard one of these voices, unlike and voice in far off, asking if it "was anywhere near Sidon?"—evidently some one lost like himself. He answered in a voice that seemed quite as unreal and as faint, and turned in the direction from which it came. There was a light moving like a will-o'-the-wisp far before him, yet below him as if coming out of the depths of the earth. It must be fancy, but he would see—ah!

He had fallen violently forward, and at the same moment felt his revolver leap from his breast pocket like a living thing, and an instant after explode upon the rock where it struck, blindingly illuminating the declivity down which he was plunging. The sulphurous sting of burning powder was in his eyes and nose, yet in that swift revealing hash he had time to clutch the stems or a trailing vine beside him, but not to save his head from sharp contact with the same rocky ledge that had caught his pistol. The pain and shock gave way to a sickening sense of warmth at the roots of his hair. Giddy and faint his fingers relaxed, he felt himself sinking, with a languor that was half acquiescence, down, down, until, with another shock, a wild gasping for air, and a swift reaction, he awoke in the cold rushing water!

Clear and perfectly conscious now, though frantically fighting for existence with the current, he could dimly see a floating black object shooting by the shore, at times striking the projections of the bank, until in its recoil it swung hail round and drifted broadside on towards him. He was near enough to catch the frayed ends of a trailing rope that fastened the structure—which seemed to be a few logs—together. With a convulsive effort he at last gained a footing upon it, and then fell fainting along its length. It was the raft which the surveyors from the embarcadero had just abandoned.

He did not know this, nor would he have thought it otherwise strange that a raft might be part of the drift of the overflow, even had he been entirely conscious, but his senses were failing, although he was still able to keep a secure position on the raft, and to vaguely believe that it would carry him to some relief and succour. How long he lay unconscious he never knew; in his after recollections of that night, it seemed to have been haunted by dreams of passing dim banks and strange places; of a face and voice that had been pleasant to him; of a terror coming upon him as he appeared to be nearing a place like that home that he had abandoned in the lonely tules. He was roused at last by a violent headache, as if his soft felt hat had been changed into a tightening crown of iron. .Lifting his hand to his head. to tear off its covering, he was surprised to find that he was wearing no hat, but that his matted hair, stiffened and dried with blood and ooze, was clinging like a cap to his skull in the hot morning sunlight. His eyelids and lashes were glued together and weighted down by the same sanguinary plaster. He crawled to the edge of his frail raft, not without difficulty, for it oscillated and rocked strangely, and dipped his hand in the current. When he had cleared his eyes he lifted them with a shock of amazement. Creek, banks, and plain had disappeared; he was alone on a bend of the tossing bay of San Francisco!

His first and only sense—cleared by fasting and quickened by reaction—was one of infinite relief. He was not only free from, the vague terrors of the preceding days and nights, but his whole past seemed to be lost and sunk for ever in this illimitable expanse. The low plain of Tasajara, with its steadfast monotony of light and shadow, had sunk beneath another level, but one that glistened, sparkled, was instinct with varying life, and moved and even danced below him. The low palisades of regularly recurring tules that had fenced in, impeded, but never relieved the blankness of his horizon, were for ever swallowed up behind him. All trail of past degradation, all record of pain and suffering, all footprints of his wandering and misguided feet were smoothly wiped out in that obliterating sea. He was physically helpless and he felt it; he was in danger, and he knew it—but he was free!

Haply there was but little wind and the sea was slight. The raft was still intact so far as he could judge, but even in his ignorance he knew it would scarcely stand the surges of the lower bay. Like most Californians who had passed the straits of

Carquinez at night in a steamer, he did not recognize the locality, nor even the distant peak of Tamalpais. There were a few dotting sails that seemed as remote, as uncertain, and as unfriendly as sea-birds. The raft was motionless, almost as motionless as he was in his cramped limbs and sun-dried, stiffened clothes. Too weak to keep an upright position, without mast, stick, or oar to lift a signal above that vast expanse, it seemed impossible for him to attract attention. Even his pistol was gone.

Suddenly, in an attempt; to raise himself, he was struck by a flash so blinding that it seemed to pierce his aching eyes and brain and turned him sick. It appeared to come from a crevice between the logs at the further end of the raft. Creeping painfully towards it he saw that it was a triangular slip of highly polished metal that he had hitherto overlooked. He did not know that it was a "flashing" mirror used in topographical observation, which had slipped from the surveyors' instruments when they abandoned the raft, but his excited faculties instinctively detected its value to him. He lifted it, and, facing the sun, raised it at different angles with his feeble arms. .But the effort was too much for him; the raft presently seemed to be whirling with his movement, and he again fell.

"Ahoy there!"

The voice was close upon—in his very ears. He opened his eyes. The sea still stretched emptily before him; the dotting sails still unchanged and distant. Yet a strange shadow lay upon the raft. He turned his head with difficulty. On the opposite side—so close upon him as to be almost over his head,—the great white sails of a schooner hovered above him like the wings of some enormous sea-bird. Then a heavy boom swung across the raft, so low that it would have swept him away had he been in an upright position; the sides of the vessel grazed the raft and she fell slowly on. A. terrible fear of abandonment took possession of him, he tried to speak, but could, not. The vessel moved further away, but the raft followed! He could see now it was being held by a boat-hook—could see the odd, eager curiosity on two faces that were raised above the taffrail, and with that sense of relief his eyes again closed in unconsciousness.

A feeling of chilliness, followed by a grateful sensation of drawing closer under some warm covering, a stinging taste in his mouth of fiery liquor and the aromatic steam of hot coffee, were his first returning sensations. His head and neck were swathed in coarse bandages, and his skin stiffened and smarting with soap. He was lying in a rude berth under a half deck from which he could see the sky and the bellying sail, and presently a bearded face filled with rough and practical concern that peered down upon him.

"Halloo! coming round, eh? Hold on!"

The next moment the stranger had leaped down beside Elijah. He seemed to be an odd mingling of the sailor and ranchero with the shrewdness of a seaport trader.

"Hullo, boss! What was it? A free fight, or a wash out?"

"A wash out!"[Footnote 1: A mining term for the temporary inundation of a claim by flood; also used for the sterilizing effect of flood on fertile soil.] Elijah grasped the idea as an inspiration. Yes, his cabin had been inundated, he had taken to a raft, had been knocked off twice or thrice, and had lost everything—even his revolver.

The man looked relieved. "Then it ain't a free fight, nor havin' your crust busted and bein' robbed by beach combers, eh?"

"No," said. Elijah with his first faint smile.

"Glad o' that," said the man bluntly. "Then thar ain't no police business to tie up to in 'Firsco? We were stuck thar a week once just because we chanced to pick up a feller who'd been found gagged and then thrown overboard by wharf thieves. Had to dance attendance at court thar and lost our trip." He stopped and looked half-pathetically at the prostrate Elijah. "Look yer! ye ain't just dyin' to go ashore now and see yer friends and send messages, are ye?"

Elijah shuddered inwardly, but outwardly smiled faintly as he replied, "No!"

"And the tide and wind jest servin' us now, ye wouldn't mind keepin' straight on with us this trip?"

"Where to?" asked Elijah.

"Santy Barbara."

"No," said Elijah, after a moment's pause. "I'll go with you."

The man leaped to his feet, lifted his head above the upper deck, shouted "Let her go free, Jerry!" and then turned gratefully to his passenger. "Look yer! A wash out is a wash out, I reckon, put it any way you like; it don't put anything back into the land, or anything back into your pocket afterwards, eh? No! And yer well out

of it, pardner! Now there's a right smart chance for location jest back of Santy .Bar-
bara, where thar ain't no God-forsaken titles to overflow; and. ez far as the land
and licker lies ye 'needn't take any water in yours' ef ye don't want it. You kin start
fresh thar, pardner, and brail up. What's the matter with you, old man, is only fever
'n' agur ketched in them tules? I kin see it in your eyes. .Now you hold on whar you
be till I go forrard and see everything taut, and then I'll come back and we'll have
a talk.

And they did. The result of which was that at the end of a week's tossing and
sea-sickness, Elijah Curtis was landed at Santa Barbara, pale, thin, but self-contained and resolute. And having found favour in the eyes of the skipper of the Kitty
Hawk, general trader, lumber dealer, and ranchman, a week later he was located on
the skipper's land and installed in the skipper's service. And from that day, for five
years, Sidon and Tasajara knew him no more.

CHAPTER IV

IT was part of the functions of John Milton Harkutt to take down the early
morning shutters and. sweep out the store for his father each day before going to
school. It was a peculiarity of this performance that he was apt to linger over it,
partly from the fact that it put on the evil hour of lessons, partly that he imparted
into the process a purely imaginative and romantic element gathered from his latest novel-reading. In this he was usually assisted by one or two schoolfellows on
their way to school, who always envied him his superior menial occupation. To go
to school, it was felt, was a common calamity of boyhood that called into play only
the simplest forms of evasion, whereas to take down actual shutters in a bonâ fide
store, and wield a real broom that raised a palpable cloud of dust, was something
that really taxed the noblest exertions. And it was the morning after the arrival of
the strangers that John Milton stood on the verandah of the store ostentatiously
examining the horizon, with his hand shading his eyes, as one of his companions
appeared.

"Hollo, Milt! wot yer doin'?"

John .Milton started dramatically, and then violently dashed at one of the shutters and began to detach it. "Ha!" he said hoarsely. "Clear the ship for action! Open the ports! On deck there! Steady, you lubbers!" In an instant his enthusiastic school-fellow was at his side attacking another shutter. "A long, low schooner bearing down upon us! Lively, lads, lively!" continued John Milton, desisting a moment to take another dramatic look at the distant plain. "How does she head now?" he demanded fiercely.

"Sou' by sou'-east, sir," responded the other boy, frantically dancing before the window. "But she'll weather it."

They then each wrested another shutter away, violently depositing them, as they ran to and fro, in a rack at the corner of the verandah. Added to an extraordinary and unnecessary clattering with their feet, they accompanied their movements with a singular hissing sound, supposed to indicate in one breath the fury of the elements, the bustle of the eager crew, and the wild excitement of the coming conflict. When the last shutter was cleared away, John Milton, with the cry "Man the starboard guns!" dashed into the store, whose floor was marked by the muddy footprints of yesterdays buyers, seized a broom and began to sweep violently. A cloud of dust arose, into which his companion at once precipitated himself with another broom and a loud bang! to indicate the somewhat belated sound of cannon. For or a few seconds the two boys plied their brooms desperately in that stifling atmosphere, accompanying each long sweep and putt of dust out of the open door with the report of explosions and loud ha! s of defiance, until not only the store, but the verandah were obscured with a cloud which the morning sun struggled vainly to pierce. In the midst of this tumult and dusty confusion—happily unheard and unsuspected in the secluded domestic interior of the building—a shrill little voice arose from the road.

"Think you're mighty smart, don't ye?"

The two naval heroes stopped in their imaginary fury, and, as the dust of conflict cleared away, recognized little Johnny Peters gazing at them with mingled-. inquisitiveness and envy.

"Guess ye don't know what happened down the run last night," he continued impatiently. "Lige Curtis got killed, or killed hisself! Blood all over the rock down thar. Seed, it myseff. Dad picked up his six-shooter—one barrel gone off. My dad was the first to find it out, and he's bin to Squire Kerby tellin' him."

The two companions, albeit burning with curiosity, affected indifference and pre-knowledge.

"Dad sez your father druv Lige outer the store lass night! Dad sez your father's sponsible. Dad sez your father ez good ez killed him. Dad sez the squire 'll set the constable on your father. Yah! But here the small insulter incontinently fled, pursued by both the boys. Nevertheless, when he had made good his escape, John Milton showed neither a disposition to take up his former nautical rôle, nor to follow his companion to visit the sanguinary scene of Elijah's disappearance. He walked slowly back to the store and continued his work of sweeping and putting in order with an abstracted regularity, and no trace of his former exuberant spirits.

The first one of those instinctive fears which are common to imaginative children, and often assume the functions of premonition, had taken possession of him. The oddity of his father's manner the evening before, which had only half consciously made its indelible impression on his sensitive fancy, had recurred to him with Johnny Peters's speech. He had no idea of literally accepting the boy's charges: he scarcely understood their gravity; but he had a miserable feeling that his father's anger and excitement last night was because he had been discovered hunting in the dark for that paper of Lige Curtis's It was Lige Curtis's paper, for he had seen it lying there. A sudden dreadful conviction came over him that he must never, never let any one know that he had seen his father take up that paper; that he must never admit it, even to him. It was not the boy's first knowledge of that attitude of hypocrisy which the grown-up world assumes towards childhood, and in which the innocent victims eventually acquiesce with a Machiavellian subtlety that at last avenges them,—but it was his first knowledge that that hypocrisy might not be so innocent. His father had concealed something from him, because it was not right.

But if childhood does not forget, it seldom broods and is not above being diverted. And the two surveyors—of whose heroic advent in a raft John Milton had only heard that morning—with their travelled ways, their strange instruments and stranger talk, captured his fancy. Kept in the background by his sisters when visitors came, as an unpresentable feature in the household, he however managed to linger near the strangers when, in company with Euphemia and Clementina, after breakfast they strolled beneath the sparkling sunlight in the rude garden enclosure along the sloping banks of the creek. It was with the average brother's supreme

contempt that he listened, to his sisters "practisin'" upon the goodness of these superior beings; it was with an exceptional pity that he regarded the evident admiration of the strangers in return. felt that in the case of Euphemia, who sometimes
evinced a laudable curiosity in his pleasures, and a flattering ignorance of his reading, this might be pardonable; but what any one could find in the useless statuesque
Clementina passed his comprehension. Could they not see at once that she was "just
that kind of person" who would lie abed in the morning, pretending she was sick, in
order to make Phemie do the house-work, and make him, John .Milton, clean her
boots and fetch things for her? Was it not perfectly plain to them that her present
sickening politeness was solely with a view to extract from them caramels, rock
candy and gum drops, which she would meanly keep herself, and perhaps some
"buggy-riding" later? Alas! John Milton, it was not! For standing there with her
tall, perfectly proportioned figure outlined against a willow, an elastic branch of
which she had drawn down by one curved arm above her head, and on which she
leaned—as everybody leaned against something in Sidon—the two young men saw
only a straying goddess in a glorified rosebud print. Whether the clearly cut profile
presented to Rice, or the full face that captivated Grant, each suggested possibilities of position, pride, poetry and passion that astonished while it fascinated them.
By one of those instincts known only to the freemasonry of the sex, Euphemia lent
herself to this advertisement of her sister's charms by subtle comparison with her
own prettinesses, and thus combined against their common enemy, man.

"Clementina, certainly, is perfect to keep her supremacy over mat pretty little
sister," thought Rice.

"What a fascinating little creature to hold her own against that tall, handsome
girl," thought Grant.

"They're takin' stock o' them two fellers so as to gabble about 'em when their
backs is turned," said John Milton, gloomily to himself, with a dismal premonition
of the prolonged tea-table gossip he would be obliged to listen to later.

"We were very fortunate to make a landing at all last night," said Rice, looking
down upon the still swollen current, and then raising his eyes to Clementina. "Still
more fortunate to make it where we did. I suppose it must have been the singing
that lured us on to the bank—as, you know, the sirens used to lure people—only
with less disastrous consequences."

John Milton here detected three glaring errors; first it was not Clementina who had sung; secondly, he knew that neither of his sisters had ever read anything about sirens, but he had; thirdly, that the young surveyor was glaringly ignorant of local phenomena and. should be corrected.

"It's nothin' but the current," he said with that feverish youthful haste that betrays a fatal experience of impending interruption. It's always leavin' drift and rubbish from everywhere here. There ain't anythin' that's chucked into the creek above that ain't bound to fetch, up on this bank. Why there was two sheep and a dead hoss here long afore you thought of coming!" He did not understand why this should provoke the laughter that it did, and to prove that he had no ulterior meaning, added with pointed politeness: "So it isn't your fault, you know—you couldn't help it;" supplementing this with the distinct courtesy, "Otherwise you wouldn't have come."

"But it would seems that your visitors are not all as accidental as your brother would imply, and one, at least, seems to have been expected this evening. You remember you thought we were a Mr. Parmlee," said Mr. Rice looking at Clementina.

It would be strange indeed, he thought, if the beautiful girl were not surrounded by admirers. But without a trace of self-consciousness or any change in her reposeful face, she indicated her sister with a slight gesture, and said: "One of Phemie's friends. He gave her the accordion. She's very popular."

"And I suppose you are very hard to please?" he said with a tentative smile.

She looked at him with her large, clear eyes, and that absence of coquetry or changed expression in her beautiful face which might have stood for indifference or dignity as she said: "I don't know. I am waiting to see."

But here Miss Phemie broke in saucily with the assertion that Mr. Parmlee might not have a railroad in his pocket, but that at least he didn't have to wait for the Flood to call on young ladies, nor did he usually come in pairs, for all the world as if he had been let out of Noah's Ark, but on horseback, and like a Christian by the front door. All this provokingly and bewitchingly delivered, however, and with a simulated exaggeration that was incited apparently more by Mr. Lawrence Grant's evident enjoyment of it, than by any desire to defend the absent Parmlee.

"But where is the front door?" asked Grant laughingly.

The young girl pointed to a narrow, zig-zag path that ran up the bank beside the house until it stopped at a small picketed gate on the level of the road and store.

"But I should think it would be easier to have a door and private passage through the store," said Grant.

"We don't," said the young lady pertly.

"We have nothing to do with the store. I go in to see paw sometimes when he s shutting up and there s nobody there, but Clem has never set foot in it since we came. It's bad enough to have it, and the lazy loafers that hang around it as near to us as they are; but paw built the house in such a fashion that we ain't troubled by their noise, and we might be t'other side of the creek as far as our having to come across them. And because paw has to sell pork and floour, we haven't any call to go there and watch him do it."

The two men glanced at each other. This reserve and fastidiousness were something rare in a pioneer community. Harkutt's manners certainly did not indicate that he was troubled by this sensitiveness; it must have been some individual temperament of his daughters. Stephen felt his respect increase for the goddess-like Clementina; Mr. Lawrence Grant looked at Miss Phemie with a critical smile.

"But you must be very limited in your company, he said; "or is Mr. Parmlee not a customer of your father's?"

"As Mr. Parmlee does not come to us through the store, and don't talk trade to me, we don't know," responded Phemie saucily.

"But have you no lady acquaintances—neighbours—who also avoid the store and enter only at the straight and narrow gate up there?" continued Grant mischievously, regardless of the uneasy, half-reproachful glances of Rice.

But Phemie, triumphantly oblivious of any satire, answered promptly: "If you mean the Pike County Billingses who live on the turn-pike road as much as they do off it, or the six daughters of that Georgia Cracker who wear men's boots and hats, we haven't."

"And Mr. Parmlee, your admirer?" suggested Rice. "Hasn't he a mother or sisters here.?"

"Yes, but they don't want to know us, and have never called here."

The embarrassment of the questioner at this unexpected reply, which came from the faultless lips of Clementina, was somewhat mitigated by the fact that the young woman s voice and manner betrayed neither annoyance nor anger.

Here, however, Harkutt appeared from the house with the information that he had secured two horses for the surveyors and their instruments, and that he would himself accompany them a part of the way on their return to Tasajara Creek, to show them the road. His usual listless deliberation had given way to a certain nervous but uneasy energy. If they started at once it would be better, before the loungers gathered at the store and confused them with lazy counsel and languid curiosity. He took it for granted that Mr. Grant wished the railroad survey to be a secret, and he had said nothing, as they would be pestered with questions. "Sidon was inquisitive—and old-fashioned. The benefit its inhabitants would get from the railroad would not prevent them from throwing obstacles in its way at first; he remembered the way they had acted with a proposed wagon road—in fact, an idea of his own, something like the railroad; he knew them thoroughly, and if he might advise them, it would be to say nothing here until the thing was settled.

"He evidently does not intend to give us a chance," said Grant good-humouredly to his companion, as they turned to prepare for their journey; "we are to be conducted in silence to the outskirts of the town like horse-thieves."

"But you gave him the tip for himself, said Rice reproachfully; "you cannot blame him for wanting to keep it."

"I gave it to him in trust for his two incredible daughters," said Grant with a grimace. "But hang it! if I don't believe the fellow has more concern in it than I imagined."

"But isn't she perfect?" said Rice, with charming abstraction.

"Who?"

"Clementina, and so unlike her father."

"Discomposingly so," said Grant quietly. "One feels in calling her 'Miss Harkutt' as if one were touching upon a manifest indiscretion. But here comes John Milton. Well, my lad, what can I do for you?"

The boy, who had been regarding them from a distance with wistful and curious eyes as they replaced their instruments for the journey, had gradually approached them. After a moment's timid hesitation he said, looking at Grant: "You don't know anybody in this kind o' business," pointing to the instruments, "who'd like a boy about my size?"

"I'm afraid not, J.M.", said Grant cheerfully, without suspending his operation. "The fact is, you see, it s not exactly the kind of work for a boy of your size."

John Milton was silent for a moment, shifting himself slowly from one leg to another as he watched the surveyor. After a pause he said. "There don't seem to be much show in this world for boys o' my size. There don't seem to be much use for 'em any way." This not bitterly, but philosophically, and even politely, as if to relieve Grant's rejection of any incivility.

"Really you quite pain me, John Milton," said Grant, looking up as he tightened a buckle. "I never thought of it before, but you're right."

"Now," continued the boy slowly, "with girls it's just different. Girls of my size everybody does things for. There's Clemmy—she's only two years older nor me, and don t know half that I do, and yet she kin lie about all day, and hasn't to get up to breakfast. And Phemie—who's jest the same age, size, and weight as me—maw and paw lets her do everything she wants to. And so does everybody. And so would you."

"But you surely don't want to be like a girl?" said Grant, smiling.

It here occurred to John Milton's youthful but not illogical mind that this was not argument, and he turned disappointedly away. As his father was to accompany the strangers a short distance he, John Milton, was to-day left in charge of the store. That duty, however, did not involve any pecuniary transactions—the taking of money or making of change—but a simple record on a slate behind the counter of articles selected by those customers whose urgent needs could not wait Mr. Harkutt's return. Perhaps on account of this degrading limitation, perhaps for other reasons, the boy did not fancy the task imposed upon him. The presence of the idle loungers who usually occupied the arm-chairs near the stove, and occasionally the counter, dissipated any romance with which he might have invested his charged; he wearied of the monotony of their dull gossip, but mostly he loathed the attitude of hypercritical counsel and instruction which they saw fit to assume towards him at such moments. "Instead o' lazin' thar behind the counter when your father ain't here to see ye, John," remarked Billings from the depths of his arm-chair a few moments after Harkutt had ridden away, "ye orter be bustlin' round, dustin the shelves. Ye'll never come to anythin' when you're a man ef you go on like that. Ye never heard o' Harry Clay—that was called 'the Mill-Boy of the Slashes'—sittin' down doin' nothin' when he was a boy."

I never heard of him loafin' round in a grocery store when he was growned up either," responded John Milton darkly.

"P'raps you reckon he got to be a great man by standin' up sassin' his father's customers, said Peters angrily. "I kin tell ye, young man, if you was my boy—"

"If I was your boy, I'd be playin' hookey instead of goin' to school, jest as your boy is doin' now," interrupted John Milton, with a literal recollection of his quarrel and pursuit of the youth in question that morning.

And undignified silence on the part of the adults followed, the usual sequel to those passages; Sidon generally declining to expose itself to the youthful Harkutt's terrible accuracy of statement.

The men resumed their previous lazy gossip about Elijah Curtis's disappearance, with occasional mysterious allusions in a lower tone, which the boy instinctively knew referred to his father, but which either from indolence or caution—the two great conservators of Sidon—were never formulated distinctly enough for his relentless interference. The morning sunshine was slowly thickening again in. an indolent mist that seemed to rise from the saturated plain. A. stray lounger shuffled over from the blacksmith's shop to the store to take the place of another idler who had joined an equally lethargic circle around the slumbering forge. A dull intermittent sound of hammering came occasionally from the wheelwright's shed—at sufficiently protracted intervals to indicate the enfeebled progress of Sidon's vehicular repair. A yellow dog left his patch of sunlight on the opposite side of the way and walked deliberately over to what appeared to be more luxurious quarters on the verandah; was manifestly disappointed but not equal to the exertion of returning, and sank down with blinking eyes and regretful sigh without going further. A procession of six ducks got well into a line for a laborious march past the store, but fell out at the first mud puddle and gave it up. A highly nervous but respectable hen, who had ventured upon the verandah evidently against her better instincts, walked painfully on tip-toe to the door, apparently was met by language which no mother of a family could listen to, and retired in strong hysterics. A little later the sun became again obscured, the wind arose, rain fell, and the opportunity for going indoors and doing nothing was once more availed of by all Sidon.

It was afternoon when Mr. Harkutt returned. He did not go into the store, but entered the dwelling from the little picket-gate and steep path. There he called a family council in the sitting-room as being the most reserved and secure. Mrs. Harkutt, sympathizing and cheerfully ready for any affliction, still holding a dust-cloth in her hand, took her seat by the window, with Phemie breathless and sparkling at one side of her, while Clementina, all faultless profile and repose, sat on the other. To Mrs. Harkutt's motherly concern at John Milton's absence, it was pointed out that he was wanted at the store—was a mere boy, anyhow, and could not be trusted. Mr. Harkutt, a little ruddier from weather, excitement, and. the unusual fortification of a glass of liquor, a little more rugged in the lines of his face, and with an odd ring of defiant self-assertion in his voice, stood before them in the centre of the room.

He wanted them to listen to him carefully, to remember what he said, for it was important; it might be a matter of "lawing" hereafter—and lie couldn't be always repeating it to them—he would have enough to do. There was a heap of it that, as womenfolks, they couldn't understand, and weren't expected to. But he'd got it all clear now, and what he was saying was Gospel. He'd always known to himself that the only good that could ever come to Sidon would come by railroad. When those fools talked wagon road he had said nothing, but he had his own ideas; he had worked for that idea without saying anything to anybody; that idea was to get possession of all the land along embarcadero which nobody cared for, Lige Curtis was ready to sell for a song. Well, now, considering what had happened, lie didn't mind telling them that he had been gradually getting possession of it, little by little, paying Lige Curtis in advances and instalments, until it was his own. They had heard what those surveyors said; how that it was the only fit terminus for the railroad. Well, that land, and that waterfront, and the terminus were his! And all from his own foresight and prudence.

It is needless to say that this was not the truth. But it is necessary to point out that this fabrication was the result of his last night's cogitations and his morning's experience. He had resolved upon a bold course. He had reflected that his neighbours would be more ready to believe in and to respect a hard, mercenary, and speculative foresight in his taking advantage of Lige's necessities than if he had—as was the case—merely benefited by them through an accident of circumstance and good humour. In the latter case he would be envied and hated, in the former he would be envied and feared. By logic of circumstance the greater wrong seemed to be less obviously offensive than the minor fault. It was true that it involved, the doing of something he had not contemplated, and the certainty of exposure Lige ever returned, but he was nevertheless resolved. The step from passive to active wrongdoing is not only easy, it is often a relief; it is that return to sincerity which we all require-Howbeit, it gave that ring of assertion to Daniel Harkutt's voice already noted, which most women like, and only men are prone to suspect or challenge. The incompleteness of his statement was, for the same reason, overlooked by his feminine auditors.

"And what is it worth, dad?" asked Phemie eagerly

"Grant says I oughter get at least ten thousand dollars for the site of the terminus from the company, but of course I shall hold on to the rest of the land. The moment they get the terminus there, and the depôt and wharf built, I can get my own price and buyers for the rest. Before the year is out, Grant thinks it ought to go up ten per cent, on the value of the terminus, and that a hundred thousand."

"Oh, dad!" gasped Phemie, frantically clasping her knees with both hands as if to perfectly assure herself of this good fortune.

Mrs. Harkutt audibly murmured, "Poor dear Dan'll, and. stood, as it were, sympathetically by, ready to commiserate the pains and anxieties of wealth as she had those of poverty. Clementina alone remained silent, clear-eyed, and unchanged.

"And to think it all came through them!" continued Phemie. "I always had an idea that Mr. Grant was smart, dad. And it was real kind of him to tell you."

"I reckon father could have found it out without them. I don't know why we should be beholden to them particularly. I hope he isn't expected to let them think that he isn't bound to consider them our intimate friends just because they happened to drop in here at a time when his plans have succeeded."

The voice was Clementina's, unexpected but quiet, unemotional and convincing. "It seemed," as Mrs. Harkutt afterwards said, "as if the child had already touched that hundred thousand." Phemie reddened with a sense of convicted youthful extravagance.

"You needn't fear for me," said .Harkutt, responding to Clementina's voice as if it were an echo of his own, and instinctively recognizing an unexpected ally. "I've got my own ideas of this thing, and what s to come of it. I've got my own ideas of openin' up that property and showin' its resources. I'm goin' to run it my own way. I'm goin' to have a town along the embarcadero that'll lay over any town in Contra-Costa. I'm goin' to have the court-house and county seat there, and a couple of hotels as good as any in the Bay. I'm goin' to build that wagon road through here that those lazy louts slipped up on, and carry it clear over to Five Mile Corner, and open up the whole Tasajara Plain!"

They had never seen him look so strong, so resolute, so intelligent and handsome. A dimly prophetic vision of him in a black broadcloth suit and gold watch-chain addressing a vague multitude, as she remembered to have seen the Hon. Stanley Riggs of Alasco at the "Great Barbecue," rose before Phemie's blue enraptured eyes. With the exception of Mrs. Harkutt,—equal to any possibilities on the part of her husband, they had honestly never expected it of him. They were pleased with their father's attitude in prosperity, and felt that perhaps he was not unworthy of being proud of them hereafter.

"But we're goin' to leave Sidon," said Phemie, "ain't we, paw?"

"As soon as I can run. up a new house at the embarcadero," said Harkutt peevishly," and that's got to be done mighty quick if I want to make a show to the company and be in possession."

"And that's easier for you to do, dear, now that Lige's disappeared," said Mrs. Harkutt, consolingly.

"What do ye mean by that? What the devil are ye talkin' about?" demanded Harkutt suddenly with unexpected exasperation.

"I mean that that drunken Lige would be mighty poor company for the girls if he was our only neighbour," remarked Mrs. Harkutt, submissively.

Harkutt, after a fixed survey of his wife, appeared mollified. The two girls, who were both mindful of his previous outburst the evening before, exchanged glances which implied that his manners needed correction for Prosperity.

"You'll want a heap o' money to build there, Dan'l," said. Mrs. Harkuttt in plaintive diffidence.

"Yes! Yes!" said Harkutt impatiently. "I've kalkilated all that, and I'm goin' to 'Frisco to-morrow to raise it and. put this bill of sale on record." He half drew Elijah Curtis's paper from his pocket but paused and put it back again.

"Then that was the paper, dad," said Phemie triumphantly.

"Yes," said her father regarding her fixedly, "and you know now why I didn't want anything said about it last night—nor even now."

"And Lige had just given it to you! Wasn't it lucky?"

"He hadn't just given it to me!" said her father with another unexpected outburst. "God Almighty! ain't I tellin' you all the time it was an old matter! But you jabber, jabber all the time and don't listen! Where's John .Milton?" It had occurred to him that the boy might have read the paper—as his sister had—while it lay unheeded on the counter.

"In the store—you know. You said he wasn't to hear anything of this, but I'll call him," said Mrs. Harkutt, rising eagerly.

"Never mind," returned her husband, stopping her reflectively, "best leave it as it is; if it's necessary I'll tell him. But don't any of you say anything, do you hear?"

Nevertheless a few hours later, when the store was momentarily free of loungers, and Harkutt had relieved his son of his monotonous charge, he made a pretence, while abstractedly listening to an account of the boy's stewardship, to look through a drawer as if in search of some missing article.

You didn't see anything of a paper I left somewhere about here yesterday? he asked carelessly.

"The one you picked up when you came in last night?" said the boy with discomposing directness.

Harkutt flushed slightly and drew his breath between his set teeth. Not only could he place no reliance upon ordinary youthful inattention, but he must be on his guard against his own son as from a spy! But he restrained himself..

"I don't remember," he said with, affected deliberation, "what it was I picked up. Do you? Did you read it?"

The meaning of his father's attitude instinctively flashed upon the boy. He had read the paper, but he answered, as he had already determined, "No."

An inspiration seized Mr. Harkutt. He drew Lige Curtis's bill of sale from his pocket, and opening it before John Milton said: "Was it that?"

"I don't know," said the boy. "I couldn't tell." He walked away with, affected carelessness, already with a sense of playing some part like his father and pretended to whistle for the dog across the street. Harkutt coughed ostentatiously, put the paper back in his pocket, set one or two boxes straight on the counter, locked the drawer and disappeared into the back passage. John Milton remained standing in the doorway looking vacantly out. But he did not see the dull familiar prospect beyond. He only saw the paper his father had opened and unfolded before him. It was the same paper he had read last night. But there were three words written there that were not there before! After the words "Value received" there had been a blank. He remembered that distinctly. This was filled in by the words: "Five hundred dollars." The handwriting did not seem like his father's, nor yet entirely like Lige Curtis's. What it meant he did not know—he would not try to think. He should forget it, as he had tried to forget what had happened before, and he should never tell it to any one!

There was a feverish gaiety in his sisters' manner that afternoon that he did not understand; short colloquies that were suspended with ill-concealed impatience when he came near them, and resumed when he was sent, on equally palpable excuses, out of the room. He had been accustomed to this exclusion, when there were strangers present, but it seemed odd to him now, when the conversation did not even turn upon the two superior visitors who had been there, and of whom he confidently expected they would talk. Such fragments as he overheard were always in the future tense, and. referred to what they intended to do. His mother, whose affection for him had always been shown in excessive and depressing commiseration of him in even his lightest moments, that afternoon seemed to add a prophetic and Cassandra-like sympathy for some vague future of his that would require all her ministration. You won't need them new boots, Milty dear, in the changes that may be comin' to ye; so don't be bothering poor father in his worriments over his new plans."

"What new plans, mommer?" asked the boy abruptly. "Are we goin' away from here?"

"Hush, dear, and don't ask questions that's enough for grown folks to worry over, let alone a boy like you. Now be good"—a quality in Mrs. Harkutt's mind synonymous with ceasing from troubling—"and after supper, while I'm in the parlour with your father and sisters, you kin sit up here by the fire with your book."

"But," persisted the boy in a flash of inspiration, "is popper goin' to join in business with those surveyors—a surveyin'?"

"No, child, what an idea! Run away there—and mind!—don't bother your father."

Nevertheless John Milton's inspiration had taken a new and characteristic shape. All this, he reflected, had happened since the surveyors came—since they had weakly displayed such a shameless and unmanly interest in his sisters! It could, have but one meaning. He hung around the sitting-room and passages until he eventually encountered Clementina, taller than ever, evidently wearing a guilty satisfaction in her face, engrafted upon that habitual bearing of hers which he had always recognized as belonging to a vague but objectionable race whose members were individually known to him as "a proudy."

"Which of those two surveyor fellows is it, Clemmy?" he said with an engaging smile, yet halting at a strategic distance.

"Is what?"

"Wot you're goin to marry."

"Idiot!"!

"That ain't tellin' which," responded the boy darkly.

Clementina swept by him into the sitting-room, where he heard her declare that really that boy was getting too low and vulgar for anything." Yet it struck him that being pressed for further explanation she did not specify why. This was "girls' meanness!"

Howbeit he lingered late in the road that evening, hearing his father discuss with the search-party that had followed the banks of the creek, vainly looking for further traces of the missing Lige, possibility of his being living or dead, of the body having been carrried away by the current to the bay, or turning up later in some distant marsh when the spring came with low water. One—who had been to his cabin beside the embarcadero, —reported that it was, as had been long suspected, barely habitable, and contained neither books, papers, nor records which would indicate his family or friends. It was a God-forsaken, dreary, worthless place; he wondered how a white man could ever expect to make a living there. If Elijah never turned up again it certainly would be a long time before any squatter would think of taking possession of it. John Milton knew instinctively, without looking up, that his father's eyes were fixed upon him, and he felt himself constrained to appear to be abstracted in gazing down the darkening road. Then he heard his father say, with what he felt was an equal assumption of carelessness: "Yes, I reckon I've got somewhere a bill of sale of that land that I had to take from Lige for an old bill, but I kalkilate that's all I'll ever see of it."

Rain fell again as the darkness gathered, but he still loitered on the road and the sloping path of the garden, filled with a hail resentful sense of wrong, and hugging with gloomy pride an increasing sense of loneliness and of getting dangerously wet. The swollen creek still whispered, murmured and swirled beside the bank. At another time he might have had wild ideas of emulating the surveyors on some extempore raft and so escaping his present dreary home existence; but since the disappearance of Lige, who had always excited an odd boyish antipathy in his heart, although he had never seen him, he shunned the stream contaminated with the missing man's unheroic fate. Presently the light from the open window of the sitting-room glittered on the wet leaves and sprays where he stood, and the voices of the family conclave came fitfully to his ear. They didn't want him there. They had never thought of asking him to come in. Well!—who cared? And he wasn't going to be bought oil with a candle and a seat by the kitchen fire. No!

Nevertheless he was getting wet to no purpose. There was the tool-house and carpenter's shed near the bank; its floor was thickly covered with sawdust and pinewood shavings, and there was a mouldy buffalo skin which he had once transported thither from the old wagon bed. There, too, was his secret cache of a candle in a bottle, buried with other piratical treasures in the presence of the youthful refers, who consented to be sacrificed on the spot in buccaneering fashion to complete the unhallowed rites. He unearthed the candle, lit it, and clearing away a part of the shavings stood it up on the floor. He then brought a prized, battered, and coverless volume from a hidden recess in the rafters, and lying down with the buffalo robe over him, and his cap in his hand ready to extinguish the light at the first footstep of a trespasser, gave himself up—as he had given himself up, I fear, many other times—to the enchantment of the page before him.

The current whispered, murmured, and sang unheeded at his side. The voices of his mother and sisters, raised at times in eagerness or expectation of the future, fell upon his unlistening ears. For with the spell that had come upon him, the mean walls of his hiding place melted away; the vulgar steam beside him might have been that dim, subterraneous river down which Sinbad and his bale of riches were swept out of the Cave of Death to the sunlight of life and fortune, so surely and so simply had it transported him beyond the cramped and darkened limits of his present life. He was in the better world of boyish romance—of gallant deeds and high emprises; of miraculous atonement and devoted sacrifice; of brave men, and those rarer, impossible women—the immaculate conception of a boy's virgin heart. What mattered it that behind that glittering window his mother and sisters grew feverish and excited over the vulgar details of their real but baser fortune? From the dark tool-shed by the muddy current John Milton, with a battered dogs'-eared chronicle, soared on the wings of fancy far beyond their wildest ken!

CHAPTER V

PROSPERITY had settled upon the plains of Tasajara. Not only had the embarcadero emerged from the tules of Tasajara Creek as a thriving town of steamboat wharves, warehouses, and outlying mills and factories, but in five years the transforming railroad had penetrated the great plain itself and revealed its undeveloped fertility. The low-lying lands that had been yearly overflowed by the creek, now, drained and cultivated, yielded treasures of wheat and barley that were apparently inexhaustible. Even the helpless indolence of Sidon had been surprised into activity and change. There was nothing left of the straggling settlement to recall its former aspect. The site of Harkutt's old store and dwelling was lost and forgotten in the new mill and granary that rose along the banks of the creek. Decay leaves ruin and traces for the memory to linger over; prosperity is unrelenting in its complete and smiling obliteration of the past.

But Tasajara City, as the embarcadero was now called, had no previous record, and even the former existence of an actual settler like the forgotten Elijah Curtis was unknown to the present inhabitants. It was Daniel Harkutt's idea carried out in Daniel Harkutt's land, with Daniel Harkutt's capital and energy. But Daniel Harkutt had become Daniel Harcourt, and Harcourt Avenue, Harcourt Square, and Harcourt House, ostentatiously proclaimed the new spelling of his patronymic. When the change was made, and for what reason; who suggested it, and under what authority, were not easy to determine, as the sign on his former store had borne nothing but the legend, "Goods and Provisions" and his name did not appear on written record until after the occupation of Tasajara; but it is presumed that it was at the instigation of his daughters, and there was no one to oppose it. Harcourt was a pretty name for a street, a square, or a hotel; even the few in Sidon who had called it Harkutt admitted that it was an improvement quite consistent with, the change from the fever-haunted tules and sedges of the creek to the broad, level, and handsome squares of Tasajara City.

This might have been the opinion of a visitor at the Harcourt House, who arrived one summer afternoon from the Stockton boat, but whose shrewd, half-critical, half-professional eyes and quiet questionings betrayed some previous knowledge of the locality. Seated on the broad verandah of the Harcourt House, and gazing out on the well-kept green and young eucalyptus trees of the Harcourt Square or Plaza, he had elicited a counter question from a prosperous-looking citizen who had been lounging at his side.

"I reckon you look ez if you might have been here before, stranger."

"Yes," said the stranger quietly, "I have been. But it was when the tules grew in the square opposite, and the tide of the creek washed them."

"Well," said the Tasajaran, looking curiously at the stranger, "I call myself a pioneer of Tasajara. My name's Peters—of Peters and Co.—and those warehouses along the wharf, where you landed just now, are mine, but I was the first settler on Harcourt's land, and built the next cabin after him. I helped to clear out them tules and dredged the channels yonder. I took the contract with Harcourt to build the last fifteen miles o' railroad, and put up that depot for the company. Perhaps you were here before that?"

"I was," returned the stranger quietly.

I say, said Peters, hitching his chair a little nearer to his companion, "you never knew a kind of broken down feller, called Curtis—Lige Curtis—who once squatted here and sold his right to Harkutt? He disappeared—it was allowed he killed hisself, but they never found his body, and, between you and me, I never took stock in that story. You know Harcourt holds under him, and all Tasajara rests on that title."

"I've heard so," assented the stranger carelessly, "but I never knew the original settler. Then Harcourt has been lucky?"

"You bet. He's got three minions right about here, or within this quarter section, to say nothing of his outside speculations."

"And lives here?"

"Not for two years. That's his old house across the plaza, but his women folks live mostly in 'Frisco and New York, where he s got houses too. They say they sorter got sick of Tasajara after his youngest daughter ran off with a feller."

"Hallo!" said the stranger with undisguised interest. "I never heard of that! You don't mean that she eloped—"he hesitated.

"Oh, it was a square enough marriage. I reckon too square to suit some folks; but the fellow hadn't nothin', and wasn't worth shucks—a sort of land surveyor, doin' odd jobs, you know; and the old man and old woman were agin it, and the tother daughter worse of all. It was allowed here—you know how women folks talk!-—that the surveyor had been sweet on Clementina, but had got tired of being played by her, and took up with Phemie out o spite. Anyhow, they got married, and Harcourt gave them to understand they couldn't expect anything from him. P'raps that's why it didn't last long, for only about two months ago she got a divorce from Rice and came back to her family again."

"Rice?" queried the stranger, "was that her husband's name, Stephen Rice?"

"I reckon! You knew him?"

"Yes—when the tide came up to the tules, yonder," answered the stranger musingly. "And the other daughter—I suppose she has made a good match, being a beauty and the sole heiress?"

The Tasajaran made a grimace. "Not much! I reckon she's waitin' for the Angel Gabriel—there ain't another good, enough to suit her here. They say she's had most of the big men in California waitin' in a line with their offers, like that cue the fellows used, to make at the 'Frisco Post Office, steamer days—and she with nary a letter or answer for any of them."

"Then Harcourt doesn't seem to have been as fortunate in. his family affairs as in his Speculations?"

Peters uttered a grim laugh. "Well, I reckon you know all about his son's stampeding with that girl last spring?"

"His son?" interrupted the stranger. "Do you mean the boy they called John Milton? Why, he was a mere child!"

"He was old enough to run away with a young woman that helped in his mother's house, and marry her afore a Justice of the Peace, The old man just snorted with rage, and swore he'd have the marriage put aside, for the boy was under age. He said it was a put-up job of the girl's; that she was older by two years, and only wanted to get what money might be coming some day, but that they'd never see a red cent of it. Then, they say, John Milton up and sassed the old man to his face, and allowed that he wouldn't take his dirty money if he starved first, and that if the old man broke the marriage he'd marry her again next year; that true love and honourable poverty were better nor riches, and a lot more o that stuff he picked out o' them ten cent novels he was allus reading. My woman folks say that he actually liked the girl, because she was the only one in the house that was ever kind to him; they say the girls were just raging mad at the idea o' havin' a hired gal who had waited on 'em as a sister-in-law, and they even got old Mammy Harcourt's back up by sayin' that John's wife would want to rule the house, and run her out of her own kitchen. Some say he shook them, talked back to 'em mighty sharp, and held his head a heap higher nor them. Anyhow, he's livin' with his wife somewhere in 'Frisco, in a shanty on a sand lot, and workin' odd jobs for the newspapers. No! takin' it by and large—it don't look as if Harcourt, had run his family to the same advantage that he has his land."

"Perhaps he doesn't understand them as well," said the stranger smiling.

"Mor'n likely the material ain't thar, or ain't as vallyble for a new country," said Peters grimly. "I reckon the trouble is that he lets them two daughters run him, and the man who lets any woman or women do that, let's himself in for all their meannssses, and all he gets in return is a woman's result—show!"

Here the stranger, who was slowly rising from his chair with the polite suggestion of reluctantly tearing himself from the speaker's spell, said: "And Harcourt spends most of his time in San Francisco, I suppose?"

"Yes! but to-day he's here to attend a directors meeting and the opening of the Free Library and Tasajara Mall. I saw the windows open, and the blinds up in his house across the plaza as I passed just now."

The stranger had by this time quite effected his courteous withdrawal. "Good afternoon, Mr. Peters, he said, smilingly lifting his hat, and turned away.

Peters, who was obliged to take his legs off the chair, and half rise to the stranger's politeness, here reflected that he did not know his interlocutor's name and business, and that he had really got nothing in return for his information. This must be remedied. As the stranger passed through the hall into the street, followed, by the unwonted civilities of the spruce hotel clerk and the obsequious attentions of the negro porter, Peters stepped to the window of the office. "Who was that man who just passed out?" he asked.

The clerk stared in undisguised astonishment. "You don't mean to say you didn't know who he was—all the while you were talking to him?"

"No," returned. Peters, impatiently.

"Why, that was Professor Lawrence Grant!— the Lawrence Grant—don't you know?—the biggest scientific man and recognized expert on the Pacific slope. Why, that's the man whose single word is enough to make or break the biggest mine or claim going! That man!—why, that's the man whose opinion's worth thousands, for it carries millions with it—and can't be bought. That's him who knocked the bottom out-er El Dorado last year, and next day sent Eureka up booming ! Ye remember that, sure?"

"Of course—but—" stammered Peters.

"And to think you didn't know him!" repeated the hotel clerk wonderingly. "And here I was reckoning you were getting points from him all the time! Why, some men would have given a thousand dollars for your chance of talking to him— yes!—of even being seen talking to him. Why, old Wingate once got a tip on his Prairie Flower lead worth five thousand dollars while just changing seats with him in the cars and passing the time of day, sociable like. Why, what did you talk about?"

Peters, with a miserable conviction that he had thrown away a valuable opportunity in mere idle gossip, nevertheless endeavoured to look mysterious as he replied, "Oh, business gin'rally." Then in the faint hope of yet retrieving his blunder he inquired, "How long will he be here?"

"Don't know. I reckon he and Harcourt's got something on hand. He just asked if he was likely to be at home or at his office. I told him I reckoned at the house, for some of the family—I didn't get to see who they were—drove up in a carriage from the 3.40 train while you were sitting there."

Meanwhile the subject of this discussion, quite unconscious of the sensation he had created, or perhaps like most heroes philosophically careless of it, was sauntering indifferently towards Harcourt's house. But he had no business with his former host—his only object was to pass an idle hour before his train left. fie was, of course, not unaware that he himself was largely responsible for Harcourt's success; that it was his hint which had induced the petty trader of Sidon to venture his all in Tasajara; his knowledge of the topography and geology of the plain that had stimulated Harcourt's agricultural speculations—his hydrographic survey of the creek that had made Harcourt's plan of widening the channel to commerce practical and profitable. This he could not help but know. But that it was chiefly owing to his own clear, cool, farseeing, but never visionary, scientific observation—his own accurate analysis, unprejudiced by even a savant's enthusiasm, and uninfluenced by any personal desire of greed or gain—that Tasajara City had risen from the stagnant tules, was a speculation that had never occurred to him. There was a much more uneasy consciousness of what he had done in Mr. Harcourt's face a few moments later, when his visitor's name was announced, and it is to be feared that if that name had been less widely honoured and respected than it was, no merely grateful recollection of it would have procured Grant an audience. As it was, it was with a frown and a touch of his old impatient asperity that he stepped to the threshold of an adjoining room and caned, "Clemmy!"

Clementina appeared at the door.

"There's that man Grant in the parlour. What brings him here I wonder? Who does he come to see?"

"Who did he ask for?"

"Me—but that don't mean anything."

"Perhaps he wants to see you on some business."

"No. That isn't his high-toned style. He makes other people go to him for that, he said bitterly. "Anyhow don't you think its mighty queer his coming here after his friend—for it was he who introduced Rice to us—had behaved so to your sister, and caused all this divorce and scandal?"

"Perhaps he may know nothing about it; he and Rice separated long ago, even before Grant became so famous. We never saw much of him, you know, after we came here. Suppose you leave him to me I'll see him."

Mr. Harcourt reflected. "Didn't he use to be rather attentive to Phemie?"

Clementina shrugged her shoulders carelessly. "I dare say—but I don't think that now—"

"Who said anything about now?" retorted her father, with a return of his old abruptness. After a pause he said: "I'll go down and see him first—and then send for you. You can keep him for the opening and dinner, if you like."

Meantime Lawrence Grant, serenely unsuspicious of these domestic confidences, had been shown into the parlour—a large room furnished in the same style as the drawing-room of the hotel he had just quitted. He had ample time to note that it was that wonderful Second Empire furniture which he remembered that the early San Francisco pioneers in the first Hush of their wealth had imported directly from France, and which for years after gave an unexpected foreign flavour to the western domesticity and a tawdry gilt equality to saloons and drawing-rooms, public and private. But he was observant of a corresponding change in Harcourt, when a moment later lie entered the room. That individuality—which had kept the former shopkeeper of Sidon distinct from, although perhaps not superior to, his customers, was strongly marked. He was perhaps now more nervously alert than then; he was certainly more impatient than before—but that was pardonable in a man of large affairs and action. Grant could not deny that he seemed improved—rather perhaps that the setting of fine clothes, cleanliness, and the absence of petty worries, made his characteristics respectable. That which is ill-breeding in homespun, is apt to become mere eccentricity in purple and fine linen; Grant felt that Harcourt jarred on him less than he did before, and was grateful without superciliousness. Harcourt, relieved to find that Grant was neither critical nor aggressively reminiscent, and above all not inclined to claim the credit of creating him and Tasajara, became more confident, more at his ease, and, I fear, in proportion more unpleasant. It is the repose and not the struggle of the parvenu that confounds us.

"And you, Grant—you have made yourself famous, and, I hear, have got pretty much your own prices for your opinions ever since it was known that you—you—er—were connected with the growth of Tasajara."

Grant smiled; he was not quite prepared for this; but it was amusing and would pass the time. He murmured, a sentence of half ironical deprecation, and Mr. Harcourt continued:—

"I haven't got my San Francisco house here to receive you in, but I hope some day, sir, to see you there. We are only here for the day and night, but if you care to attend the opening ceremonies at the new hall we can manage to give you dinner afterwards. You can escort my daughter Clementina—she's here with me."

The smile of apologetic decimation which had begun to form on Grants, lips was suddenly arrested. "Then your daughter is here?" he asked, with unaffected interest.

"Yes—she is in fact a patroness of the library and sewing circle, and takes the greatest interest in it. The Rev. Doctor Pilsbury relies upon her for everything. She runs the society, even to the training of the young ladies, sir. You shall see their exercises."

This was certainly a new phase of Clementina's character. Yet why should she not assume the rôle of .Lady Bountiful with the other functions of her new condition? "I should have thought Miss Harcourt would have found this rather difficult with her other social duties, lie said, "and would have left it to her married sister. He thought it better not to appear as if avoiding reference to Euphemia, although quietly ignoring her late experiences. Mr. Harcourt was less easy in his response.

"Now that Euphemia is again with her own family," he said ponderously, with an affectation of social discrimination that was in weak contrast to his usual direct business astuteness, "I suppose she may take her part in these things, but just now she requires rest. You may have heard some rumour that she is going abroad for a time? The fact is she hasn't the least intention of doing so, nor do we consider there is the slightest reason for her going. He paused as if to give great emphasis to a statement that seemed otherwise unimportant. "But here's Clementina coming and I must get you to excuse me. I've to meet the trustees of the church in ten minutes, but I hope she'll persuade you to stay, and I'll see you later at the hall."

As Clementina entered the room her father vanished and, I fear, as completely dropped out of Mr. Grant's mind. For the daughter's improvement was greater than her fathers, yet so much more refined as to be at first only delicately perceptible. Grant had been prepared for the vulgar enhancement of fine clothes and personal adornment, for the specious setting of luxurious circumstances and surroundings, for the aplomb that came from flattery and conscious power. But he found none of these; her calm individuality was intensified rather than subdued; she was dressed simply, with an economy or ornament, rich material, and jewellery, but an accuracy of taste that was always dominant. Her plain grey merino dress, beautifully fitting her figure, suggested with its pale blue facings some uniform as of the charitable society she patronized. She came towards him with a graceful movement of greeting, yet her face showed no consciousness of the interval that had elapsed since they met; he almost fancied himself transported back to the sitting-room at Sidon with the monotonous patter of the leaves outside, and the cool moist breath of the bay and alder coming in at the window.

"Father says that you are only passing through Tasajara to-day as you did through Sidon five years ago," she said with a smiling earnestness that he fancied however was the one new phase of her character. "But I won't believe it! At least we will not accept another visit quite as accidental as that, even though you brought us twice the good fortune you did then. You see, we have not forgotten it if you have, Mr. Grant. And unless you want us to believe that your fairy gifts will turn some day to leaves and ashes, you will promise to stay with us to-night, and let me show you some of the good we have done with them. Perhaps you don't know, or don't want to know, that it was I who got up this 'Library and Home Circle of the Sisters of Tasajara' which we are to open to-day. And can you imagine why? You remember—or have you forgotten?—that you once affected to be concerned at the social condition of the young ladies on the plains of Sidon. Well, Mr. Grant, this is gotten up in order that the future Mr. Grants who wander may find future Miss Billingses who are worthy to converse with them and entertain them, and who no longer wear men's hats and live on the public road."

It was such a long speech for one so taciturn as he remembered Clementina to have been; so unexpected in tone considering her father's attitude towards him, and so unlocked for in its reference to a slight incident of the past, that Grant's critical contemplation of her gave way to a quiet and grateful glance of admiration. How could he have been so mistaken in her character? He had always preferred the out-spoken Euphemia, and yet why should he not have been equally mistaken in her? Without having any personal knowledge of Rice's matrimonial troubles—for their intimate companionship had not continued after the survey—he had been inclined to blame him; now he seemed to find excuses for him. He wondered if she really had liked him as Peters had hinted; he wondered if she knew that he, Grant, was no longer intimate with him, and knew nothing of her affairs. All this while he was accepting her proffered hospitality and sending to the hotel for his luggage. Then he drilled, into a conversation, which he had expected would be brief, point-less and confined to a stupid, résumé of their mutual and social progress since they had left Sidon. But here he was again, mistaken; she was talking familiarly of present social topics, of things that she knew clearly and well, without effort or attitude. She had been to New York and Boston for two winters; she had spent the previous summer at Newport; it might have been her whole youth, for the fluency, accuracy, and familiarity of her detail, and the absence of provincial enthusiasm. She was going abroad probably in the spring. She had thought of going to winter in Italy, but she would wait now until her sister was ready to go with her. Mr. Grant of course knew that Euphemia was separated from Mr. Rice—no!—not until her father told him? Well—the marriage had been a wild and foolish thing for both out Euphemia was back again with them in the San Francisco house; she had talked of coming to Tasajara to-day, perhaps she might be there to-night. And, good heavens! it was actually three o' clock already, and they must start at once for the Hall. She would go and get her hat and return instantly.

It was true; he had been talking with her an hour—pleasantly, intelligently, and yet with a consciousness of an indefinite satisfaction beyond all this. It must have been surprise at her transformation, or his previous misconception of her character. He had been watching her features and wondering why he had ever thought them expressionless. There was also the pleasant suggestion—common to humanity in such instances—that he himself was in some way responsible for the change; that it was some awakened sympathy to his own nature that had breathed into this cold and faultless statue the warmth of life. In an odd flash of recollection he remembered how, five years ago, when Rice had suggested to her that she was "hard to please," she had replied that she didn't know, but that she was waiting to see. It did not occur to him to wonder why she had not awakened then, or if this awakening had anything to do with her own volition. It was not probable that they would meet again after to-day, or if they did, that she would not relapse into her former self and fail to impress him as she had now. But—here she was—a paragon of feminine promptitude—already standing doorway, accurately gloved and booted, and wearing a demure grey hat that modestly crowned her decorously elegant figure.

They crossed the plaza, side by side, in the still garish sunlight that seemed to mock the scant shade of the youthful eucalyptus trees, and presently fell in with the stream of people going in their direction. The former daughters of Sidon, the

Billingses, the Peterses, and Wingates, were there, bourgeoning and expanding in
the glare of their new prosperity, with silk and gold; there were newer faces still,
and pretty ones—for Tasajara as a "Cow County" had attracted settlers with large
families—and there were already the contrasting types of East and West. Many
turned to look after the tall figure of the daughter of the Founder of Tasajara—a
spectacle lately rare to the town; a few glanced at her companion, equally notice-
able as a stranger. Thanks, however, to some judicious preliminary advertising from
the hotel clerk, Peters, and .Daniel Harcourt himself, by the time Grant and Miss
Harcourt had reached the Hall his name and fame were already known, and speculation had already begun whether this new stroke of Harcourt's shrewdness might
not unite Clementina to a renowned and profitable partner.

The Hall was in one of the further and newly opened suburbs, and its side and
rear windows gave immediately upon the outlying and inimitable plain of Tasajara.
It was a tasteful and fair seeming structure of wood, surprisingly and surpassingly
new. In fact that was its one dominant feature; nowhere else had youth and freshness ever shown itself as unconquerable and all-conquering. The spice of virgin
woods and trackless forests still rose from its pine floors, and breathed from its outer
shell of cedar that still oozed its sap, and redwood that still dropped its life-blood.
Nowhere else were the plastered walls and ceilings as white and dazzling in their
unstained purity, or as redolent of the outlying quarry in their clear cool breath of
lime and stone. Even the turpentine of fresh and spotless paint added to this sense
of wholesome germination, and as the clear and brilliant Califonian sunshine swept
through the open windows west and east, suffusing the whole palpitating structure
with its searching and resistless radiance, the very air seemed filled with the aroma
of creation.

The fresh colours of the young Republic, the bright blazonry of the newest
State, the coat of arms of the infant County of Tasajara—(a vignette of sunset-tules
cloven by the steam of an advancing train)—hanging from the walls, were all a part
of this invincible juvenescence. Even the newest silks, ribbons and prints of the
latest holiday fashions made their first virgin appearance in the new building as if
to consecrate it, until it was stirred by the rustle of youth, as with the sound and
movement of budding spring.

A strain from the new organ—whose heart, however, had prematurely learned its own bitterness,—and a thin, clear, but somewhat shrill chanting from a choir of young ladies were followed by a prayer from the Rev. Mr. Pilsbury. Then there was a pause of expectancy, and Grant's fair companion, who up to that moment had been quietly acting as guide and cicerone to her father's guest, excused herself with a little grimace of mock concern and was led away by one of the committee. Grant's usually keen eyes were wandering somewhat abstractedly over the agitated and rustling field of ribbons, flowers and feathers before him, past the blazonry of banner on the walls, and through the open windows to the long sunlit levels beyond, when he noticed a stir upon the raised, dais or platform at the end of the room, where the notables of Tasajara were formally assembled. The mass of black coats suddenly parted and drew back against the wall to allow the coming forward of a single graceful figure. A thrill of nervousness as unexpected as unaccountable passed over him as he recognized Clementina. In the midst of a sudden silence she read the report of the committee from a paper in her hand, in a clear, untroubled voice—the old voice of Sidon—and formally declared the building opened! The sunlight nearly level, streamed through the western window across the front of the platform where she stood, and transfigured her slight but noble figure. The hush that had fallen upon the Hall was as much the effect of that tranquil, ideal presence as of the message with which it was charged. And yet that apparition was as inconsistent with the clear, searching light which helped to set it off as it was with, the broad new blazonry of decoration, the yet unsullied record of the white walls, or even the frank, animated and pretty faces that looked upon it. Perhaps it was some such instinct that caused the applause which hesitatingly and tardily followed her from the platform to appear polite and half-restrained rather than spontaneous.

Nevertheless Grant was honestly and sincerely profuse in his congratulations. "You were far cooler and far more self-contained than I should have been in your place," he said, "than in fact I actually was, only as your auditor. But I suppose you have done it before?"

She turned her beautiful eyes on his wonderingly. "No—this is the first time I ever appeared in public—not even at school, for even there A. was always a private pupil."

"You astonish me," said Grant; "you seemed like an old hand at it."

"Perhaps I did, or rather as if I. didn't think anything of it myself—and that no doubt is why the audience didn't trunk anything of it either."

So she had noticed her cold reception, and yet there was not the slightest trace of disappointment, regret, or wounded vanity in her tone or manner. "You must take me to the refreshment-room now," she said pleasantly, "and help me to look after the young ladies who are my guests. I'm afraid there are still more speeches to come, and father and Mr. Pilsbury are looking as if they confidently expected something more would be 'expected' of them."

Grant at once threw himself into the task assigned to him with his natural gallantry, and a certain captivating playfulness which he still retained. Perhaps he was the more anxious to please in order that his companion might share some of his popularity, for it was undeniable that Miss Harcourt still seemed to excite only a constrained politeness among those with whom she courteously mingled. And this was still more distinctly marked by the contrast of a later incident.

For some moments the sound of laughter and greeting had risen near the door of the refreshment-room that opened upon the central nail, and there was a perceptible movement of the crowd particularly of youthful male Tasajara—in that direction. It was evident that it announced the unexpected arrival of some popular resident. Attracted like the others, Grant turned and saw the company making way for the smiling, easy, half-saucy, half-complacent entry of a handsomely dressed young girl. As she turned from time to time to recognize with rallying familiarity or charming impertinence some of her admirers, there was that in her tone and gesture which instantly recalled to him the past. It was unmistakably Euphemia! is eyes instinctively sought Clementina's. She was gazing at him with such a grave, penetrating look—half doubting, half wistful—a look so unlike her usual unruffled calm—that he felt strangely stirred. But the next moment, when she rejoined him, the look had entirely gone. "You have not seen my sister since you were at Sidon, I believe?" she said quietly. "She would be sorry to miss you." But Euphemia and her train were already passing them on the opposite side of the long table. She had evidently recognized Grant, yet the two sisters were looking intently into each other s eyes when he raised his own. Then Euphemia met his bow with a momentary accession of colour, a coquettish wave of her hand across the table, a slight exaggeration of her usual fascinating recklessness, and smilingly moved away. He turned to Clementina, but here an ominous tapping at the further end of the long table revealed the fact that Mr. Harcourt was standing on a chair with oratorical possibilities in his face and attitude. There was another forward movement in the crowd and—silence. In that solid, black broadclothed, respectable figure, that massive watch-chain, that white waistcoat, that diamond pin glistening in the satin cravat, Euphemia might have seen the realization of her prophetic vision at Sidon five years before.

He spoke for ten minutes with a fluency and comprehensive businesslike directness that surprised Grant. He was not there, he said, to glorify what had been done by himself, his family, or his friends in Tasajara. Others who were to follow him might do that, or at least might be better able to explain and expatiate upon the advantages of the institution they had just opened, and its social, moral, and religious effect upon the community. He was there as a business man to demonstrate to them—as he had always done and always hoped to do—the money value of improvement; the profit—if they might choose to call it—of well-regulated and properly calculated speculation. The plot of land upon which they stood, of which the building occupied only one-eighth, was bought two years be-fore for ten thousand dollars. When the plans of the building were completed a month afterwards, the value of the remaining seven-eighths had risen enough to defray the cost of the entire construction. He was in a position to tell them that only that morning the adjacent property, subdivided and laid out in streets and building-plots, had been admitted into the corporate limits of the city; and that on the next anniversary of the building they would approach it through an avenue of finished dwellings! An outburst of applause followed the speaker's practical climax; the fresh young faces of his auditors glowed with invincible enthusiasm; the afternoon trade-winds, freshening over the limitless plain beyond, tossed the bright banners at the windows as with sympathetic rejoicing, and a few odorous pine shavings, overlooked in a corner in the hurry of preparation, touched by an eddying zephyr crept out and rolled in yellow ringlets across the floor.

The Reverend Doctor Pilsbury arose in a more decorous silence. He had listened approvingly, admiringly, he might; say even reverently, to the preceding speaker. But although his distinguished friend had, with his usual modesty, made light of his own services and those of his charming family, he, the speaker, had not risen to sing his praises. No; it was not in this Hall, projected by his foresight and raised by his liberality, in this town, called into existence by his energy and stamped by his attributes; in this county, developed by his genius and sustained by his capital—ay, in this very State whose grandeur was made possible by such giants as he—it was not in any of these places that it was necessary to praise Daniel Harcourt, or that a panegyric of him would be more than idle repetition. Nor would he, as that distinguished man had suggested, enlarge upon the social, moral, and religious benefits of the improvement they were now celebrating. It was written on the happy, innocent faces, in the festive garb, in the decorous demeanour, in the intelligent eyes that sparkled around him—in the presence of those of his parishioners whom he could meet as freely here to-day as in his own church on Sunday. What then could he say? What then was there to say? Perhaps he should say nothing if it were not for the presence of the young before him.—He stopped and fixed his eyes paternally on the youthful Johnny Billings, who with a half dozen other Sunday school scholars, had been marshalled before the reverend speaker—And what was to be the lesson they were to learn from it? They had heard what had been achieved by labour, enterprise, and diligence Perhaps they would believe, and naturally too, that what labour, enterprise, and diligence had done could be done again. But was that all? Was there nothing behind these qualities—which, after all, were within the reach of every one here? .Had they ever thought that back of every pioneer, every explorer, every path-finder, every founder and creator, there was still another? There was no terra incognita so rare as to be unknown to One; no wilderness so remote as to be beyond a greater ken than theirs; no waste so trackless but that One had already passed that way! Did they ever reflect that when the dull sea ebbed and flowed in the tules over the very spot where they were now standing, Who it was that also foresaw, conceived, and ordained the mighty change that would take place; Who even guided and directed the feeble means employed to work it; whose spirit moved, as in still older days of which they had read, over the face of the stagnant waters? Perhaps they had. Who then was the real pioneer of Tasajara—back of the Harcourts, the Peters, the Billingses, and Wingates? The reverend gentleman gently paused for a reply. It was given in the clear but startled accents of the half-frightened, half-fascinated Johnny Billings, in three words:

"Lige Curtis, sir!"

CHAPTER VI

THE trade wind, that blowing directly from the Golden Grate seemed to concentrate its full force upon the western slope of Russian Hill, might have dismayed any climber less hopeful and sanguine than that most imaginative of newspaper reporters and most youthful of husbands, John -Milton Harcourt. But for all that it was an honest wind and its dry, practical energy and salt-pervading breath only seemed to sting him to greater and more enthusiastic exertions, until quite at the summit of the hill and last of a straggling line of little cottages half submerged in drifting sand, he stood upon his own humble porch.

"I was thinking, coming up the hill, Loo," he said, bursting into the sitting-room, pantingly, "of writing something about the future of the hill! How it will look fifty years from now!—all terraced with houses and gardens!—and right up here a kind of Acropolis, don't you know. I had quite a picture of it in my mind just now."

A plainly-dressed young woman with a pretty face, that, however, looked as if it had been prematurely sapped of colour and vitality, here laid aside some white sewing she had in her lap, and said:

"But you did that once before, Milty, and you know the Herald wouldn't take it because they said it was a free notice of Mr. Boorem's building lots, and lie didn't advertise in the Herald. I always told you that you ought to have seen Boorem first."

The young fellow blinked his eyes with a momentary arrest of that buoyant hopefulness which was their peculiar characteristic, but nevertheless replied with undaunted cheerfulness, "I forgot. Anyhow, it's all the same, for I worked it into that 'Sunday Walk.' And it's just as easy to write it the other way, you see—looking back— down the hill, you know. Something about the old Padres toiling through the sand just before the Angelus; or as far back as Sir Francis Drake's time, and have a runaway boat's crew coming ashore to look for gold that the Mexicans had talked of. .Lord! that's easy enough! I tell you what, Loo, it's worth living up here just for the inspiration." Even while boyishly exhaling this enthusiasm he was also divesting himself of certain bundles whose contents seemed to imply that he had brought his dinner with him—the youthful Mrs. Harcourt setting the table in a perfunctory, listless way that contrasted oddly with her husband's cheerful energy.

"You haven't heard of any regular situation yet?" she asked abstractedly.

"No—not exactly," he replied. "But [buoyantly] it's a great deal better for me not to take anything in a hurry and tie myself to any particular line. Now, I'm quite free."

"And I suppose you haven't seen that Mr. Fletcher again?" she continued.

"No. He only wanted to know something about me. That's the way with them all, Loo. Whenever I apply for work anywhere it's always: 'So you're Dan'l Harcourt's son, eh? Quarrelled with the old man? Bad job; better make it up. You'll make more stickin' to him. He's worth millions!' Everybody seems to think everything of him, as if I had no individuality beyond that. I've a good mind to change my name."

"And pray what would mine be then?"

There was so much irritation in her voice that he drew nearer her and gently put his arm around her waist. "Why, whatever mine was, darling," he said with a tender smile. "You didn't fall in love with any particular name, did you, Loo?"

"No, but I married a particular one," she said quickly.

His eyelids quivered again, as if he was avoiding some unpleasantly staring suggestion she stopped.

"You know what I mean, dear," she said, with a quick little laugh. "Just because your father's an old crosspatch, you haven't lost your rights to his name and property. And those people who say you ought to make it up, perhaps know what's for the best."

"But you remember what he said of you, Loo?" said the young man with a flashing eye. "Do you think I can ever forget that?"

"But you do forget it, dear; you forget it when you go in town among fresh faces and people: when you are looking for work. You forget it when you're at wont writing your copy—for I've seen you smile as you wrote. You forget it climbing up the dreadful sand, for you were thinking just now of what happened years ago, or is to happen years to come. And I want to forget it too, Milty. I don't want to sit here all day, thinking of it, with the wind driving the sand against the window, and nothing to look at but those white tombs in Lone Mountain cemetery, and those white caps that might be gravestones too, and not a soul to talk to or even see pass by until I feel as if I were dead and buried also. If you were me—you—you—you couldn't help crying too!"

Indeed, he was very near it now. For as he caught her in his arms, suddenly seeing with a lover's sympathy and the poet's swifter imagination all that she had seen and even more, he was aghast at the vision conjured. In her delicate health and loneliness how dreadful must have been these monotonous days, and this glittering cruel sea! What a selfish brute he was! Yet as he stood there holding her, silently and rhythmically marking his tenderness and remorseful feelings by rocking her from side to side like a languid metronome, she quietly disengaged her wet lashes from his shoulder and said in quite another tone:

"So they were all at Tasajara last week?"

"Who, dear?"

"Your father and sisters."

"Yes," said John Milton, hesitatingly.

"And they've taken back your sister after her divorce?"

The staring obtrusiveness of this fact apparently made her husband's bright sympathetic eye blink as before.

"And if you were to divorce me, you would be taken back too," she added quickly, suddenly withdrawing herself with a pettish movement and walking to the window.

But he followed. "Don't talk in that way, Loo! Don't look in that way, dear! he said, taking her hand gently, yet not without a sense of some inconsistency in her conduct that jarred upon his own simple directness. "You know that nothing can part us now. I was wrong to let my little girl worry herself all alone here, but I—I—thought it was all so—so bright and free out on this hill—looking far away beyond the Golden Gate—as far as Cathay, you know, and such a change from those dismal flats of Tasajara—and that awful stretch of tules. But it's all right now. And now that I know how you feel, we'll go elsewhere."

She did not reply. Perhaps she found it difficult to keep up her injured attitude in the face of her husband's gentleness. Perhaps her attention had been attracted by the unusual spectacle of a stranger, who had just mounted the hill and was now slowly passing along the line of cottages with a hesitating air of inquiry. "He may be looking for this house—for you," she said in an entirely new tone of interest. "Run out and see. It may be some one who wants—"

"An article," said Milton cheerfully. "By Jove! he is coming here."

The stranger was indeed approaching the little cottage, and with apparently some confidence. He was a well-dressed, well-made man, whose age looked uncertain from the contrast between his heavy brown moustache and his hair, that, curling under the brim of his hat, was, almost white in colour. The young man started, and said hurriedly: "I really believe it is Fletcher—they say his hair turned white from the Panama fever."

It was indeed Mr. Fletcher who entered and introduced himself. A gentle, reserved man, with something of that colourlessness of premature age in his speech which was observable in his hair. He had heard of Mr. Harcourt from a friend who had recommended him highly. As Mr. Harcourt had probably been told, he, the speaker, was about to embark some capital in a first-class newspaper in San Francisco, and should select the staff himself. He wanted to secure only first-rate talent— but above all, youthfulness, directness, and originality. The Clarion, for that was to be its name, was to have nothing "old fogey" about it. No. It was distinctly to be the organ of Young California! This and much more from the grave lips of the elderly young man, whose speech seemed to be divided between the pretty, but equally faded, young wife, and the one personification of invincible youth present—her husband.

"But I fear I have interrupted your household duties," he said pleasantly. "You were preparing dinner. Pray go on. And let me help you I'm not a bad cook—and you can give me my reward by letting me share it with you, for the climb up here has sharpened my appetite. We can't talk as we go on."

It was in vain to protest; there was something paternal as well as practical in the camaraderie of this actual capitalist and possible Mæcenas and patron as he quietly hung up his hat and overcoat, and helped to set the table with a practised hand. Nor, as he suggested, did the conversation falter, and. before they had taken their seats at the frugal board he had already engaged John Milton Harcourt as assistant editor of the Clarion at a salary that seemed princely to this son of a millionaire! The young wife meantime had taken active part in the discussion; whether it was vaguely understood that the possession of practical and imaginative faculties precluded any capacity for business, or whether it was owing to the apparent superior maturity of Mrs. Harcourt and the stranger, it was certain that they arranged the practical details of the engagement, and that the youthful husband sat silent, merely offering his always hopeful and sanguine consent.

"You'll take a house nearer to town, I suppose?" continued Mr. Fletcher to the lady, though you've a charming view here. I suppose it was quite a change from Tasajara and your father-in-law's house? I dare say he had as fine a place there—on his own homestead—as he has here?"

Young Harcourt dropped his sensitive eyelids again. It seemed hard that he could never get away from these allusions to his father! Perhaps it was only to that relationship that he was indebted for his visitor's kindness. In his simple honesty he could not bear the thought such a misapprehension. "Perhaps, Mr. Fletcher, you do not know," he said, "that my father is not on terms with me, and that we neither expect anything nor could we ever take anything from him. Could we, Loo?" He added the useless question partly because he saw that his wife's face betrayed little sympathy with him, and partly that Fletcher was looking at her curiously, as if for confirmation. But this was another of John Milton's trials as an imaginative reporter; nobody ever seemed to care for his practical opinions or facts!

"Mr. Fletcher is not interested in our little family differences, Milty," she said, looking at Mr. Fletcher, however, instead of him. "You're Daniel Harcourt's son whatever happens."

The cloud that had passed over the young man's face and eyes did not, however, escape Mr. Fletcher's attention, for he smiled, and added gaily, "And I hope my valued lieutenant in any case. Nevertheless John Milton was quite ready to avail himself of an inspiration to fetch some cigars for his guest from the bar of the Sea-View House on the slope of the hill beyond, and thereby avoid a fateful subject. Once in the fresh air again he promptly recovered his boyish spirits. The light flying scud had already effaced the first rising" stars: the lower creeping sea-fog had already blotted out the western shore and sea; but below him to the east the glittering lights of the city seemed to start up with a new, mysterious, and dazzling brilliancy. It was the valley of diamonds that Sinbad saw lying almost at his feet! Perhaps somewhere there the light of his own fame and fortune was already beginning to twinkle!

He returned, to his humble roof joyous and inspired. As he entered the hall he heard his wife's voice and his own name mentioned, followed by that awkward, meaningless silence on his entrance which so plainly indicated that either he had been the subject of conversation or that it was not for his ears. It was a dismal reminder of his boyhood at Sidon and Tasajara. But he was too full of hope and ambition to heed it to-night, and later, when Mr. Fletcher had taken his departure, his pent-up enthusiasm burst out before his youthful partner. Had she realized that their struggles were over now, that their future was secure? They need no longer fear ever being forced to take bounty from the family; they were independent of them all! He would make a name for himself that should be distinct from his father's, as he should make a fortune that would be theirs alone. The young wife smiled. "But all that need not prevent you, dear from claiming your rights when the time comes."

"But if I scorn to make the claim or take a penny of his, Loo?"

"You say you scorn to take the money you think your father got by a mere trick—at the best—and didn't earn. And now you will be able to show you can live without it, and earn your own fortune. Well, clear, for that very reason why should you let your father and others enjoy and waste what is fairly your share? For it is your share whether it came to your father fairly or not; and if not it is still your duty, believing as you do, to claim it from him, that at least you may do with it what you choose. You might want to restore it—to—to—somebody."

The young man laughed. "But, my dear Loo! suppose that I were weak enough to claim it, do you think my father would give it up? .tie has the right, and no law could force him to yield to me more than he chooses."

"Not the law—but you could."

"I don't understand you," he said quickly.

"You could force him by simply telling him what you once told me."

John Milton drew back, and his hand dropped loosely from his wife's. The colour left his fresh young face; the light quivered for a moment and then became fixed and set in his eyes. For that moment he looked ten years her senior. "I was wrong ever to tell even you that, Loo," he said in a low voice. "You are wrong to ever remind me of it. Forget it from this moment, as you value our love and want it to live and be remembered. And forget, Loo, as I do—and ever snail—that you ever suggested to me to use my secret in the way you did just now."

But here Mrs. Harcourt burst into tears, more touched by the alteration in her husband's manner, I fear, than by any contrition for wrongdoing. Of course if he wished to withdraw his confidences from her, just as he had almost confessed he wished to withdraw his name, she couldn't help it, but it was hard that when she sat there all day long trying to think what was best for them, she should be blamed! At which the quiet and forgiving John Milton smiled remorsefully and tried, to comfort her. Nevertheless an occasional odd, indefinable chill seemed to creep across the feverish enthusiasm with which he was celebrating this day of fortune. And yet he neither knew nor suspected until long" after that his foolish wife had that night half betrayed his secret to the stranger.

The next day he presented a note of introduction from Mr. Fletcher to the business manager of the Clarion, and the following morning was duly installed in office. He did not see his benefactor again; that single visit was left in the mystery and isolation of an angelic episode. It later appeared that other and larger interests in the San José valley claimed his patron's residence and attendance; only the capital and general purpose of the paper—to develop into a party organ in the interest of his possible senatorial aspirations in due season—was furnished by him. Grateful as John Milton felt towards him, he was relieved; it seemed probable that Mr. Fletcher had selected him on his individual merits, and not as the son of a millionaire.

He threw himself into his work with his old hopeful enthusiasm, and perhaps an originality of method that was part of his singular independence. Without the student's training or restraint,—for his two years' schooling at Tasajara during his parents' prosperity came too late to act as a discipline,—he was unfettered by any rules, and guided only by an unerring instinctive taste that came near being genius. He was a brilliant and original, if not always a profound and accurate, reporter. By degrees, he became an accustomed interest to the readers of the Clarion; then an influence. Actors themselves in many a fierce drama, living lives of devotion, emotion, and picturesque incident, they had satisfied themselves with only the briefest and most practical daily record of their adventure, and even at first were dazed and startled to find that many of them had been heroes and some poets. The stealthy boyish reader of romantic chronicle at Sidon had learned by heart the chivalrous story of the emigration. The second column of the Clarion became famous even while the figure of its youthful writer, unknown and unrecognized, was still nightly climbing the sands of Russian Mill, and even looking down as before on the lights of the growing city, without a thought that he had added to that glittering constellation.

Cheerful and contented with the exercise of work, he would have been happy but for the gradual haunting of another dread which presently began to drag him at earlier hours up the steep path to his little home; to halt him before the door with the quickened breath of an anxiety he would scarcely confess to himself, and sometimes hold him aimlessly a whole day beneath his roof. For the pretty, but delicate, Mrs. Harcourt, like others of her class, had added a weak and ineffective maternity to their other conjugal trials, and one early dawn a baby was born that lingered with them scarcely longer than the morning mist and exhaled with the rising sun. The young wife regained her strength slowly—so slowly that the youthful husband brought his work at times to the house to keep her company. And a singular change had come over her one no longer talked of the past nor of his family. As if the little life that had passed with that morning mist had represented some ascending expiatory sacrifice, it seemed to have brought them into closer communion.

Yet her weak condition made him conceal another trouble that had come upon him. It was in the third month of his employment on the Clarion that one afternoon, while correcting some proofs on his chief's desk, he came upon the following editorial paragraph:—

"The played-out cant of 'pioneer genius' and 'pioneer discovery' appears to have reached its climax in the attempt of some of our contemporaries to apply it to Dan Harcourt's new Tasajara Job before the Legislature. It is perfectly well known in Harcourt's own district that, far from being a pioneer and settler himself, he simply succeeded after a fashion to the genuine work of one Elijah Curtis, an actual pioneer and discoverer, years before, while Harcourt, we believe, was keeping a frontier doggery in Sidon, and dispensing 'tangle foot' and salt junk to the hayfooted Pike Countians of his precinct. This would make him as much of the 'pioneer discoverer as the rattlesnake who first takes up board and lodgings and then possession in a prairie dog's burrow. And if the traveller's tale is true that the rattlesnake sometimes makes a meal of his landlord—the story told at Sidon may be equally credible that the original pioneer mysteriously disappeared about the time that Dan Harcourt came into the property. From which it would seem that Harcourt is not in a position for his friends to invite very deep scrutiny into his 'pioneer' achievements."

Stupefaction, a vague terror and rising anger rapidly succeeded, each other in the young man's mind as he stood mechanically holding the paper in his hand. It was the writing of his chief editor, whose easy brutality he had sometimes even boyishly admired. Without stopping to consider their relative positions he sought him indignantly and laid the proof before him. The editor laughed. .out what s that to you? You're not on terms with the old. man."

"But he is my father," said John Milton hotly.

"Look here," said the editor good-naturedly, "I'd like to oblige you, but it isn't business, you know—and this is, you understand— proprietor's business, too! Of course I see it might stand in the way of your making up to the old man afterwards and coming in for a million. Well! you can tell him it's me. Say I would put it in. Say I'm nasty—and I am!"

"Then it must go in?" said John Milton with a white face.

"You bet."

"Then I must go out." And writing out his resignation, he laid it before his chief and left.

But he could not bear to tell this to his wife when he climbed the hill that night, and he invented some excuse for bringing his work home. The invalid never noticed any change in his usual buoyancy, and indeed I fear, when he was fairly installed with his writing materials at the foot of her bed, he had quite forgotten the episode. He was recalled to it by a faint sigh.

"What is it, dear?" he said, looking up.

"I like to see you writing, Milty. You always look so happy."

"Always so happy, dear?"

"Yes. You are happy, are you not?"

"Always." He got up and kissed her. Nevertheless, when he sat down to his work again, his face was turned a little more to the window.

Another serious incident—to be also kept from the invalid—shortly followed. The article in the Clarion had borne its fruit. The third day after his resignation a rival paper sharply retorted:—"The cowardly insinuations against the record of a justly honoured capitalist," said the Pioneer, "although quite in keeping with the brazen Clarion, might attract the attentions of the slandered party, if it were not known to his friends as well as himself that it may be traced almost directly to a cast-off member of his own family, who, it seems, is reduced to haunting the back doors of certain blatant journals to dispose of his cheap wares. The slanderer is secure from public exposure in the superior decency of his relations, who refrain from airing their family linen upon editorial lines".

This was the journal to which John Milton had hopefully turned for work. When he read it there seemed but one thing for him to do—and he did it. Gentle and optimistic as was his nature, he had been brought up in a community where sincere directness of personal offence was followed by equally sincere directness of personal redress, and—he challenged the editor. The bearer of his cartel was one Jack Hamlin, I grieve to say a gambler by profession, but between whom and John Milton had sprung up an odd friendship of which the best that can be said is that it was to each equally and unselfishly unprofitable. The challenge was accepted, the preliminaries arranged. "I suppose," said jack carelessly, "as the old man ought to do something for your wife in case of accident, you've made some sort of a will?"

"I've thought of that," said John Milton dubiously, "but I'm afraid its of no use You see—" he hesitated, " I'm not of age."

"May I ask how old you are, sonny?" said Jack with great gravity.

"I'm almost twenty," said John Milton colouring.

"It isn't exactly vingt-et-un, but I'd stand on it; if I were you I wouldn't draw to such a hand,' said Jack coolly.

The young husband had arranged to be absent from his home that night, and early morning found him, with Jack, grave, but courageous, in a little hollow behind the Mission Hills, To them presently approached his antagonist jauntily accompanied by Colonel Starbottle, his second. They halted, but after the formal salutation were instantly joined by Jack Hamlin. For a few moments John Milton remained awkwardly alone—pending a conversation which even at that supreme moment he felt as being like the general attitude of his friends towards him, in its complete ignoring of himself. The next moment the three men stepped towards him. "We have come, sir," said Colonel Starbottle in his precisest speech but his jauntiest manner, "to offer you a full and ample apology—a personal apology—which only supplements that full public apology that my principal, sir, this gentleman," indicating the editor of the Pioneer, "has this morning made in the columns of his paper, as you will observe," producing a newspaper. "We have, sir," continued the Colonel loftily, "Only within the last twelve hours become aware of the— er—real circumstances of the case. We would regret that the affair had gone so far already, if it had not given us, sir, the opportunity of testifying to your gallantry. We do so gladly; and if—er—er—a few years later, Mr. Harcourt, you should ever need—a friend in any matter of this kind, I am, sir, at your service". John Milton gazed half inquiringly, half uneasily at Jack.

"It's all right, Milt," he said sotto voce. "Shake hands all round and let's go to breakfast. And I rather think that editor wants to employ you himself."

It was true, for when that night he climbed eagerly the steep homeward hill, he carried with him the written offer of an engagement on the Pioneer. As he entered the door his wife s nurse and companion met him with a serious face. There had been a strange and unexpected change in the patient's condition, and the doctor had already been there twice. As he put aside his coat and hat and entered her room it seemed to him that he had for ever put aside all else of essay and ambition beyond those four walls. And with the thought a great peace came upon him. It seemed good to him to live for her alone.

It was not for long. As each monotonous day brought the morning mist and evening fog regularly to the little hill-top where his whole being was now centred, she seemed to grow daily weaker, and the little circle of her life narrowed day by day. One morning when the usual mist appeared to have been withheld and the sun had risen with a strange and cruel brightness; when the waves danced and sparkled on the bay below, and light glanced from dazzling sails, and even the white tombs on Lone Mountain glittered keenly; when cheery voices hailing each other on the hillside came to him clearly but without sense or meaning; when earth, sky, and sea seemed quivering with life and motion, he opened the door of that one little house on which the only shadow seemed to have fallen, and went forth again into the world alone.

CHAPTER VII

MR. DANIEL HARCOURT'S town mansion was also on an eminence, but it was that gentler acclivity of fashion known as Rincon Hill, and sunned itself on a southern slope of luxury. It had been described as "princely," and "fairylike," by a grateful reporter; tourists and travellers had sung its praises in letters to their friends and in private reminiscences, for it had dispensed hospitality to most of the celebrities who had visited the coast. Nevertheless its charm was mainly due to the ruling taste of Miss Clementina Harcourt, who had astonished her father by her marvellous intuition of the nice requirements and elegant responsibilities of their position; and had thrown her mother into the pained perplexity of a matronly hen, who, among the ducks' eggs entrusted to her fostering care, had unwittingly hatched a graceful but discomposing cygnet.

Indeed, after holding out feebly against the siege of wealth at Tasajara and San Francisco, Mrs. Harcourt had abandoned herself hopelessly to the horrors of its invasion; had allowed herself to be dragged from her kitchen by her exultant daughters and set up in black silk in a certain conventional respectability in the drawing-room. Strange to say, her commiserating hospitality, or hospital-like ministration, not only gave her popularity, but a certain kind of distinction. An exaltation so sorrowfully deprecated by its possessor was felt to be a sign of superiority. She was spoken of as "motherly," even by those who vaguely knew that there was somewhere a discarded son struggling in poverty with a helpless wife, and that she had sided with her husband in disinheriting a daughter who had married unwisely. She was sentimentally spoken of as a "true wife," while never opposing a single meanness of her husband, suggesting a single active virtue, nor questioning her right to sacrifice herself and her family for his sake. With nothing she cared to affect she was quite free from affectation, and even the critical Lawrence Grant was struck with the dignity which her narrow simplicity, that had seemed small even in Sidon, attained in her palatial hall in San Francisco. It appeared to be a perfectly logical conclusion that when such unaffectedness and simplicity were forced to assume a hostile attitude to anybody, the latter must be to blame.

Since the festival of Tasajara, Mr. Grant had been a frequent visitor at Harcourt's, and was a guest on the eve of his departure from San Francisco. The distinguished position of each made their relations appear quite natural without inciting gossip as to any attraction in Harcourt's daughters. It was late one afternoon as he was passing the door of Harcourt's study that his host called him in. He found him sitting at his desk with some papers before him and a folded copy of the Clarion. With his back to the fading light of the window his face was partly in shadow.

"By the way, Grant," he began, with an assumption of carelessness somewhat inconsistent with the fact that he had just called him in, "it may be necessary for me to pull up those fellows who are blackguarding me in the Clarion"

"Why, they haven't been saying anything new?" asked Grant, laughingly, as he glanced towards the paper.

"No—that is—only a re-hash of what -they said before," returned Harcourt without opening the paper.

"Well," said Grant playfully, "you don't mind their saying that you're not the original pioneer of Tasajara, for its true: nor that that fellow Lige Curtis disappeared suddenly, for he did, if I remember rightly. But there's nothing in that to invalidate your rights to Tasajara, to say nothing of your five years' undisputed possession."

"Of course there's no legal question," said Harcourt almost sharply. "But as a matter of absurd report, I may want to contradict their insinuations. And you remember all the circumstances, don t you?"

"I should think so! Why, my dear fellow, I've told it everywhere!—here, in New York, Newport, and in London; by Jove! It's one of my best stories. How a company sent me out with a surveyor to look up a railroad and agricultural possibilities in the wilderness; how just as I found them—and a rather big thing they made, too—I was set afloat by a flood and a raft, and drifted ashore on your bank, and practically demonstrated to you what you didn't know and didn't dare to hope for—that there could be a water-way straight to Sidon from the embarcadero. I've told what a charming evening we had with you and your daughters in the old house, and how I returned your hospitality by giving you a tip about the railroad; and how you slipped out while we were playing cards to clinch the bargain for the land with that drunken fellow, Lige Curtis—"

"What's that?" interrupted Harcourt, quickly.

It was well that the shadow hid from Grant the expression of Harcourt's face, or his reply might have been sharper. As it was, he answered a little stiffly:

"I beg your pardon——"

Harcourt recovered himself. "You're all wrong!" he said, "that bargain was made long before; I never saw Lige Curtis after you came to the house. It was before that, in the afternoon," he went on hurriedly, "that he was last in my store. I can prove it." Nevertheless he was so shocked and indignant at being confronted in his own suppressions and falsehoods by an even greater and. more astounding misconception of fact, that for a moment he felt helpless. What, he reflected, if it were alleged that Lige had returned again after the loafers had gone, or had never left the store as had been said? Nonsense! There was John Milton, who had been there reading all the time, and who could disprove it. Yes, but—John Milton—was his discarded son—his enemy—perhaps even his very slanderer!

"But," said Grant quietly, "don't you remember that your daughter Euphemia said something that evening about the land Lige had offered you, and you snapped up the young lady rather sharply for letting out secrets, and then you went out? At least that's my impression."

It was, however, more than an impression; with Grant s scientific memory for characteristic details he had noticed that particular circumstance as part of the social phenomena.

"I don t know what Phemie said," returned Harcourt impatiently. "I know there was no offer pending; the land had been sold to me before I ever saw you. Why—you must have thought me up to pretty sharp practice with Curtis—eh?" he added, with a forced laugh.

Grant smiled; he had been accustomed to hear of such sharp practice among his business acquaintance, although he himself by nature and profession was incapable of it, but he had not deemed Harcourt more scrupulous than others. "Perhaps so," he said lightly, "but for Heaven's sake don't ask me to spoil my reputation as a raconteur for the sake of a mere fact or two. I assure you it's a mighty taking story as I tell it—and it don t hurt you in a business way. You re the hero of it—hang it all!

"Yes, said Harcourt, without noticing Grant's half cynical superiority, "but you'll oblige me if you won t tell it again in that way. There are men here mean enough to make the worst of it. It's nothing to me—of course—but my family—the girls, you know, are rather sensitive.

"I had no idea they even knew it—much less cared for it, said Grant, with sudden seriousness. "I dare say if those fellows in the Clarion knew that they were annoying the ladies they'd drop it. Who s the editor? Look here—leave it to me; I'll look, into it. Better that you shouldn't t appear in the matter at all."

"You understand that if it was a really serious matter, Grant," said Harcourt with a slight attitude, "I shouldn't t allow any one to take my place."

"My dear fellow, there'll be nobody called out' and no 'shooting at sight whatever is the result of my interference," returned Grant lightly. "It'll be all right." He was quite aware of the power of his own independent position and the fact that had been often appealed to before in delicate arbitration.

Harcourt was equally conscious of this, but by a strange inconsistency now felt relieved at the coolness with which Grant had accepted the misconception which had at first seemed so dangerous. If he were ready to condone what he thought was sharp practice he could not be less lenient with the real facts that might come out—of course always excepting that interpolated consideration in the bill of sale, which, however, no one but the missing Curtis could ever discover. The fact that a man of Grant's secure position had interested himself in this matter would secure him from the working of that personal vulgar jealousy which his humbler antecedents had provoked. And if, as he fancied, Grant really cared for, Clementina——

"As you like," he said, with half affected lightness, "and now let us talk of something else. Clementina has been thinking of getting up a riding party to San Mateo for Mrs. Ash wood. We must show them some civility, and that Boston brother of hers, Mr. Shipley, will have to be invited also. I can t get away, and my wife of course will only be able to join them at San Mateo in the carriage. I reckon it would be easier for Clementina if you took my place, and helped her to look after the riding party. It will need a man, and I think she'd prefer you—as you know she's rather particular—unless of course you'ld be wanted for Mrs. Ash wood or Phemie, or somebody else."

From his shadowed corner he could see that a pleasant light had sprung into Grant's eyes, although his reply was in his ordinary easy banter. "I shall be only too glad to act as Miss Clementina's vaquero and lassoo her runaways, or keep stragglers in the road."

There seemed to be small necessity, however, for this active co-operation, for when the cheerful cavalcade started from the house a few mornings later, Mr. .Lawrence Grant's onerous duties seemed to be simply confined to those of an ordinary cavalier at the side of Miss Clementina—a few paces in the rear of the party. But this safe distance gave them the opportunity of conversing without being overheard—an apparently discreet precaution.

"Your father was so exceedingly affable to me the other day that if I hadn t given you my promise to say nothing, I think I would have fallen on my knees to him then and there, revealed my feelings, asked for your hand and his blessing—or whatever one does at such a time. But how long do you intend to keep me in this suspense?"

Clementina turned her clear eyes half abstractedly upon him as if imperfectly recalling some forgotten situation. "You forget," she said, "that part of your promise was that you wouldn't even speak of it to me again without my per-mission."

"But my time is so short now. Give me some definite hope before I go. Let me believe that when we meet in New York—"

"You will find me just the same as now! Yes! I think I can promise that. Let that suffice. You said the other day you liked me because I had not changed for five years. You can surely trust that I will not alter in as many months."

"If I only knew——"

"Ah, if I only knew—if we all only knew. But we don t, Come, Mr. Grant, let it rest as it is. Unless you want to go still further back and have it as it was —at Sidon. There I think you fancied Euphemia most."

"Clementina!

"That is my name, and those people ahead of us know it already."

"You are called Clementina —but you are not merciful!"

"You are very wrong, for you might see that Mr. Shipley has twice checked his horse that he might hear what you are saying, and Phemie is always showing Mrs. Ash wood something in the landscape behind us."

All this was the more hopeless and exasperating to Grant since in the young girl's speech and manner there was not the slightest trace of coquetry or playfulness. He could not help saying a little bitterly: "I don't think that any one would imagine from your manner that you were receiving a declaration."

"But they might imagine from yours that you had the right to quarrel with me—which would be worse."

"We cannot part like this! It is too cruel to me."

"We cannot part otherwise without the risk of greater cruelty."

"But say at least, Clementina, that I have no rival? There is no other more favored suitor?"

"That is so like a man—and yet so unlike the proud one I believed you to be. Why should a man like you even consider such a possibility? If I were a man I know I couldn't". She turned upon him a glance so clear and untroubled by either conscious vanity or evasion that he was hopelessly convinced of the truth of her statement, and she went on in a slightly lowered tone, "You have no right to ask me such a question—but perhaps for that reason I am willing to answer you. There is none. Hush! For a good rider you are setting a poor example to the others, by crowding me towards the bank. Go forward and talk to Phemie and tell her not to worry Mrs. Ashwood's horse, nor race with her; I don't think he's quite safe and Mrs. Ash wood isn't accustomed to using the Spanish bit. I suppose I must say something to Mr. Shipley, who doesn't seem to understand that I'm acting as chaperone and you as captain of the party."

She cantered forward as she spoke, and Grant was obliged to join her sister, who, mounted on a powerful roan, was mischievously exciting a beautiful quaker-coloured mustang ridden by Mrs. Ash wood, already irritated by the unfamiliar pressure of the Eastern woman's hand upon his bit. The thick dust which had forced the party-of twenty to close up in two solid files across the road compelled them at the first opening in the roadside fence to take the held in a straggling gallop. Grant, eager to escape from his own discontented self by doing something for others reined in beside Euphemia and the fair stranger.

"Let me take your place until Mrs. Ashwood's horse is quieted," he half whispered to Euphemia.

"Thank you—and I suppose it does not make any matter to Clem who quiets mine," she said with provoking eyes and a toss of her head worthy of the spirited animal she was riding.

"She thinks you quite capable of managing yourself and even others," he replied with a playful glance at Shipley, who was riding some-what stiffly on the other side.

"Don't be too sure, retorted. Phemie with another dangerous look; "I may give you trouble yet."

They were approaching the first undulation of the russet plain they had emerged upon—an umbrageous slope that seemed suddenly to diverge in two defiles among the shaded hills. Grant had given a few words of practical advice to Mrs. Ashwood, and shown her how to guide her mustang by the merest caressing touch of the rein upon its sensitive neck. He had not been sympathetically inclined towards the fair stranger, a rich and still youthful widow, although he could not deny her unquestioned good breeding, mental refinement, and a certain languorous thoughtfulness that was almost melancholy, which accented her blonde delicacy. But he had noticed that her manner was politely reserved and slightly constrained towards the Harcourt's, and he had already resented it with a lover s instinctive loyalty. He had at first attributed it to a want of sympathy between Mrs. Ashwood's more intellectual sentimentalities and the Harcourts undeniable lack of any sentiment whatever. But there was evidently some other innate antagonism. He was very polite to Mrs. Ashwood; she responded with a gentlewoman's courtesy, and, he was forced to admit, even a broader comprehension of his own merits than the Harcourt girls had ever shown, but he could still detect that she was not in accord with the party.

"I am afraid you do not like California, Mrs. Ash wood? "He said pleasantly. "You perhaps find the life here too unrestrained and unconventional?"

She looked at him in quick astonishment. "Are you quite sincere? Why it strikes me that this is just what it is not. And I have so longed for something quite different. From what I have been told about the originality and adventure of everything here, and your independence of old social forms and customs, I am afraid I expected the opposite of what I've seen. Why this very party, except that the ladies are prettier and more expensively gotten up—is like any party that might have ridden out at Saratoga or New York."

"And as stupid, you would say."

"As conventional, Mr. Grant; always excepting this lovely creature beneath, me, whom I can t make out and who doesn't seem to care that I should. There! look! I told you so!"

Her mustang had suddenly bounded forward, but as Grant followed he could see that the cause was the example of Phemie, who had, in some mad freak, dashed out in a frantic gallop. A half-dozen of the younger people hilariously accepted the challenge; the excitement was communicated to the others, until the whole cavalcade was sweeping down the slope. Grant was still at Mrs. Ashwood's side, restraining her mustang and his own impatient horse when Clementina joined them. "Phemie's mare has really bolted, I fear," she said in a quick whisper, "ride on and never mind us." Grant looked quickly ahead; Phemie s roan, excited by the shouts behind her and to all appearance ungovernable, was fast disappearing with her rider. Without a word, trusting to his own good horsemanship and better knowledge of the ground, he darted out of the cavalcade to overtake her.

But the unfortunate result of this was to give further impulse to the now racing horses as they approached a point where the slope terminated in two diverging cañnons. Mrs. Ashwood gave a sharp pull upon her bit. To her consternation the mustang stopped short almost instantly—planting his two fore feet rigidly in the dust and even sliding forward with the impetus. Had her seat been less firm she might have been thrown, but she recovered herself, although in doing so she still bore upon the bit, when to her astonishment the mustang deliberately stiffened himself as if for a shock, and then began to back slowly, quivering with excitement. She did not know that her native-bred animal fondly believed that he was participating in a rodeo, and that to his equine intelligence his fair mistress had just lassooed something! In vain she urged him forward; he still waited for the shock! When the cloud of dust in which she had been enwrapped drifted away, she saw to her amazement that she was alone. The entire party had disappeared into one of the cañons—but which, one she could, not tell!

When she succeeded at last in urging her mustang forward again she determined to take the right-hand, cañon and trust to being either met or overtaken. A more practical and less adventurous nature would have waited at the point of divergence for the return of some of the party, but Mrs. Ash wood was, in truth, not sorry to be left to herself and. the novel scenery for a while, and she had no doubt but she would eventually find her way to the hotel at San Mateo, which could, not be far away, in time for luncheon.

The road was still well defined, although it presently began to wind between ascending ranks of pines and larches that marked the terraces of hills, so high that

she wondered she had not noticed them from the plains. An unmistakable suggestion of some haunting primeval solitude—a sense of the hushed and mysterious
proximity of a nature she had never known before; the strange, half intoxicating
breath of unsunned foliage and untrodden grasses and herbs all combined to exalt
her as she cantered forward. Even her horse seemed to have acquired an intelligent liberty or rather to have established a sympathy with her in his needs and her
own longings; instinctively she no longer pulled him with the curb; the reins hung
loosely on his self-arched and unfettered neck; secure in this loneliness she found
herself even talking to him with barbaric freedom. As she went on the vague hush
of all things animate and inanimate around her seemed to thicken, until she unconsciously halted before a dim and pillared wood and a vast and heathless opening on
whose mute brown lips Nature seemed to have laid the finger of silence. She forgot
the party she had left, she forgot the luncheon she was going to; more important
still she forgot that she had already left the traveled track far behind her, and,
tremulous with anticipation, rode timidly into that arch of shadow.

As her horse's hoofs fell noiselessly on the elastic moss-carpeted aisle she forgot
even more than that. She forgot the artificial stimulus and excitement of the life she
had been leading so long; she forgot the small meannesses and smaller worries of
her well-to-do experiences; she forgot herself—rather she regained a self she had
long forgotten. For in the sweet seclusion of this half-darkened sanctuary the clinging fripperies of her past slipped from her as a tawdry garment. The petted, spoiled,
and vapidly precocious girlhood which had merged into a womanhood of aimless
triumphs and meaner ambitions; the worldly but miserable triumph of a marriage
that had left her delicacy abused and her heart sick and unsatisfied; the wifehood
without home, seclusion, or maternity; the widowhood that at last brought relief,
but with it the consciousness of hopelessly wasted youth—all this seemed to drop
from her here as lightly as the winged needles or noiseless withered spray from the
dim gray vault above her head. In the sovereign balm of that woodland breath her
better spirit was restored; somewhere in these wholesome shades seemed to still
lurk what should have been her innocent and nymph-like youth, and to come out
once more and greet her. Old songs she had forgotten, or whose music had failed in
the discords of her frivolous life, sang themselves to her again in that sweet, grave
silence; girlish dreams that she had foolishly been ashamed of, or had put away

with her childish toys, stole back to her once more and became real in this tender twilight; old fancies, old fragments of verse and childish lore, grew palpable and moved faintly before her. The boyish prince who should have come was there; the babe that should have been hers was there !—she stopped suddenly with flaming eyes and indignant colour. For it appeared that a man was there too, and had just risen from the fallen tree where he had been sitting.

CHAPTER VIII

SHE had so far forgotten herself in yielding to the spell of the place and in the revelation of her naked soul and. inner nature that it was with something of the instinct of outraged modesty that she seemed to shrink before this apparition of the outer world and outer worldliness. In an instant the nearer past returned; she remembered where she was, how she had come there, who she had come from, and to whom she was returning. She could see that she had not only aimlessly wandered from the world but from the road; and for that instant she hated this man who had · reminded her of it, even while she knew she must ask his assistance. It relieved her slightly to observe that he seemed as disturbed and impatient as herself, and as he took a pencil from between his lips and returned it to his pocket he scarcely looked at her.

But with her return to the world of convenances came its repression, and with a gentlewoman's ease and modulated voice she leaned over her mustang's neck and said: "I have strayed from my party and am afraid I have lost my way. We were going to the hotel at San Mateo. Would you be kind, enough to direct me there, or show me how I can regain the road by which I came?"

Her voice and manner were quite enough to arrest him where he stood with a pleased surprise in his fresh and ingenuous face. She looked at him more closely. He was, in spite of his long silken moustache, so absurdly young; he might, in spite of that youth, be so absurdly man-like! What was he doing there? Was he a farmer's son, an artist, a surveyor, or a city clerk out for a holiday? Was there perhaps a youthful female of his species somewhere for whom he was waiting and upon whose tryst she was now breaking? Was he—terrible thought!—the outlying picket of some family picnic? His dress, neat, simple, free from ostentatious ornament, betrayed nothing. She waited for his voice.

"Oh, you have left San Mateo miles away to the right," he said with quick youthful sympathy, "at least five miles ! Where did you leave your party?"

His voice was winning, and even refined, she thought. She answered it quite spontaneously: "At a fork of two roads. I see now I took the wrong turning."

"Yes, you took the road to Crystal Spring. It's just down there in the valley, not more than a mile. You'd have been there now if you hadn't turned off at the woods."

"I couldn't help it, it was so beautiful."

"Isn't it?"

"Perfect." "And such shadows, and such intensity of colour."

"Wonderful!—and all along the ridge, looking down that defile!"

"Yes, and that point where it seems as if you had only to stretch out your hand to pick a manzanita berry from the other side of the cañon,—half a mile across!"

"Yes! and that first glimpse of the valley through the Gothic gateway of rocks."

"And the colour of those rocks—cinnamon and bronze with the light green of the Yerba buena vine splashing over them."

"Yes, but for colour did you notice that hillside of yellow poppies pouring down into the valley, like a golden Niagara?"

"Certainly? and the perfect clearness of everything."

"And yet such complete silence and repose!"

"Oh yes!

"Ah yes!"

They were both gravely nodding and shaking their heads with sparkling eyes and brightened colour, looking not at each other but at the far landscape vignetted through a lozenge-shaped wind opening in the trees. Suddenly Mrs. Ashwood straightened herself in the saddle, looked grave, lifted the reins and apparently the ten years with them that had dropped from her. But she said in her easiest well-bred tones, and a half sigh, "Then I must take the road back again to where it forks?"

"Oh, no! you can go by Crystal Spring. It's no further, and I'll show you the way. But you'd better stop and rest yourself and your horse for a little while at the

Springs Hotel. It's a very nice place. Many people ride there from San Francisco to luncheon and return. I wonder that your party didn't prefer it; and if they are looking for you as they surely must be, he said, as if with a sudden conception of her importance, "they'll come there when they find you're not at San Mateo."

This seemed, reasonable, although the process of being "fetched" and taking the five miles ride, which she had enjoyed so much alone, in company was not attractive. "Couldn't I go on at once?" she said impulsively.

"You would meet them sooner," he said thoughtfully.

This was quite enough for Mrs. Ashwood. "I think I'll rest this poor horse who is really tired," she said with charming hypocrisy, "and stop at the hotel." She saw his face brighten. Perhaps he was the son of the hotel proprietor or a youthful partner himself. "I suppose you live here?" she suggested gently. "You seem to know the place so well."

"No," he returned quickly; "I only run down here from San Francisco when I can get a day off."

A day off! He was in some regular employment. But he continued: "And I used to go to boarding-school near here, and know all these woods well."

He must be a native! How odd! She had not conceived that there might be any other population here than the immigrants; perhaps that was what made him so interesting and different from the others. "Then your father and mother live here?" she said.

His frank face, incapable of disguise, changed suddenly. "No," he said simply, but without any trace of awkwardness. Then after a slight pause he laid his hand— she noticed it was white and well-kept—on her mustang's neck, and said, "If—if— you care to trust yourself to me I could lead you and your horse down a trail into the valley that is at least a third of the distance shorter. It would save you going back to the regular road, and there are one or two lovely views that I could show you. I should be so pleased if it would not trouble you. There's a steep place or two—but I think there's no danger."

"I shall not be afraid."

She smiled so graciously, and as she fully believed, maternally, that he looked at her the second time. To his first hurried impression of her as an elegant and delicately-nurtured woman—one of the class of distinguished tourists that fashion was beginning to send thither—he had now to add that she had a quantity of fine silken-spun light hair gathered in a heavy braid beneath her gray hat; that her mouth was very delicately lipped and beautifully sensitive; that her soft skin, although just then touched with excitement, was a pale faded velvet, and seemed to be worn with ennui rather than experience; that her eyes were hidden behind a strip of gray veil whence only a faint glow was discernible. To this must still be added a poetic fancy all his own that, as she sat there, with the skirt of her gray habit falling from her long-bodiced waist over the mustang's fawn-coloured flanks, and with her slim gauntleted hands lightly swaying the reins, she looked like Queen (Guinevere in the forest. Not that he particularly fancied Queen Guinevere, or that he at all imagined himself Launcelot, but it was quite in keeping with the suggestion-haunted brain of John Milton Harcourt, whom the astute reader has of course long since recognized.

Preceding her through the soft carpeted vault with a Woodman's instinct—for there was apparently no trail to be seen—the soft inner twilight began to give way to the outer stronger day, and presently she was startled to see the clear blue of the sky before her on apparently the same level as the brown pine-tesselated floor she was treading. Not only did this show her that she was crossing a ridge of the upland, but a few moments later she had passed beyond the woods to a golden hillside that sloped towards a leafy, sheltered, and exquisitely-proportioned valley. A tiny but picturesque tower, and a few straggling roofs and gables, the flashing of a crystal stream through the leaves, and a narrow white riband of road winding behind it indicated the hostelry they were seeking. So peaceful and unfrequented. it looked, nestling between the hills, that it seemed as if they had discovered it.

With his hand at times upon the bridle, at others merely caressing her mustang's neck, he led the way; there were a few breathless places where the crown of his straw hat appeared between her horse's reins, and again when she seemed almost slipping over on his shoulder, but they were passed with such frank fearlessness and invincible youthful confidence on the part of her escort that she felt no timidity. There were moments when a bit of the charmed landscape unfolding before them overpowered them both, and they halted to gaze—sometimes without a word, or only a significant gesture of sympathy and attention. At one of those artistic manifestations Mrs. Ashwood laid her slim gloved fingers lightly but unwittingly on

John Milton's arm, and withdrew them, however, with a quick girlish apology and a foolish colour which annoyed her more than the appearance of familiarity. But they were now getting well down into the valley; the court of the little hotel was already opening before them; their unconventional relations in the idyllic world above had changed; the new ones required some delicacy of handling, and she had an idea that even the simplicity of the young stranger might be confusing.

"I must ask you to continue to act as my escort," she said laughingly; "I am Mrs. Ashwood of Philadelphia, visiting San Francisco with my sister and brother, who are, I am afraid, even now hopelessly waiting luncheon for me at San Mateo. But as there seems to be no prospect of my joining them in time, I hope you will be able to give me the pleasure of your company with whatever they may give us here in the way of refreshment."

"I shall be very happy," returned John Milton with unmistakable candour; "but perhaps some of your friends will be arriving in quest of you, if they are not already here."

"Then they will join us or wait, said Mrs,". Ashwood incisively, with her first exhibition of the imperiousness of a rich and pretty woman. Perhaps she was a little annoyed that her elaborate introduction of herself had produced no reciprocal disclosure by her companion. "Will you please send the landlord to me?" she added.

John Milton disappeared in the hotel as she cantered to the porch. In another moment she was giving the landlord her orders with the easy confidence of one who knew herself only as an always welcome and highly privileged guest, which was not without its effect. And, she added carelessly, "when everything is ready you will please tell? Mr.?"

"Harcourt," suggested the landlord promptly.

Mrs. Ashwood's perfectly trained face gave not the slightest sign of the surprise that had overtaken her. "Of course—Mr. Harcourt."

"You know he's the son of the millionaire," continued the landlord, not at all unwilling to display the importance of the habitués of Crystal Spring, "though they've quarrelled and don't get together."

"I know," said the lady languidly; "and, if anyone comes here for me, ask them to wait in the parlour until I come."

Then, submitting herself and her dusty habit to the awkward ministration of the Irish chambermaid, she was quite thrilled with a delightful curiosity. She vaguely remembered that she had heard something of the Harcourt family discord—but that was the divorced daughter surely! And this young man was Harcourt's son, and they had quarrelled! A quarrel with a frank, open, ingenuous fellow like that—a mere boy—could only be the father's fault. Luckily she had never mentioned the name of Harcourt! She would not now; he need not know that it was his father who had originated the party; why should she make him uncomfortable for the few moments they were together?

There was nothing of this in her face as she descended and joined him. He thought that face handsome, well-bred, and refined. But this breeding and refinement seemed to him—in his ignorance of the world possibly—as only a graceful concealment of a self of which he knew nothing, and he was not surprised to find that her pretty gray eyes, now no longer hidden by her veil, really told him no more than her lips. He was a little afraid of her, and now that she had lost her naïve enthusiasm he was conscious of a vague remorsefulness for his interrupted work in the forest. What was he doing here? He who had avoided the cruel, selfish world of wealth and pleasure—a world that this woman represented—the world that had stood apart from him in the one dream of his life—and had let Loo die! His quickly responsive face darkened.

"I am afraid I really interrupted you up there," she said gently, looking in his face with an expression of unfeigned concern; "you were at work of some kind, I know. And I have very selfishly thought only of myself. But the whole scene was so new to me, and I so rarely meet any one who sees things as I do, that I know you will forgive me." She bent her eyes upon him with a certain soft timidity. "You are an artist?"

"I am afraid not," he said, colouring and smiling faintly; "I don't think I could draw a straight line."

"Don't try to; they're not pretty, and the mere ability to draw them straight or curved doesn't make an artist. But you are a lover of nature, I know, and from what I have heard you say I believe you can do what lovers cannot do—make others feel as they do—and that is what I call being an artist. You write? You are a poet?"

"Oh, dear no," he said with a smile, half of relief and half of naïve superiority. "I'm a prose writer—on a daily newspaper."

To his surprise she was not disconcerted; rather a look of animation lit up her face as she said brightly, "Oh, then, you can of course satisfy my curiosity about something. You know the road from San Francisco to the Cliff House. Except for the view of the sea lions when one gets there it's stupid; my brother says it's like all the San Francisco excursions—a dusty drive with a julep at the end of it. Well, one day we were coming back from a drive there, and when we were beginning to wind along the brow of that dreadful staring Lone Mountain Cemetery I said I would get out and walk, and avoid the obtrusive glitter of those tombstones rising before me all the way. I pushed open a little gate and passed in. Once among these funereal shrubs and cold statuesque lilies everything was changed; I saw the staring tombstones no longer, for like them, I seemed to be always facing the sea. The road had vanished; everything had vanished but the endless waste of ocean below me, and the last slope of rock and sand. It seemed to be the fittest place for a cemetery— this end of the crumbling earth——this beginning of the eternal sea. There! don't think that idea my own, or that I thought of it then. No,—I read it all afterwards, and that's why I'm telling you this."

She could not help smiling at his now attentive face, and went on: "Some days afterwards I got hold of a newspaper four or six months old, and there was a description of all that I thought I had seen and felt—only far more beautiful and touching as you shall see, for I cut it out of the paper and have kept it. It seemed to me that it must be some personal experience—as if the writer had followed some dear friend there—although it was with the unostentation and indefiniteness of true and delicate feeling. It impressed me so much that I went back there twice or thrice, and always seemed to move to the rhythm of that beautiful funeral march—and I am afraid, being a woman, that I wandered around among the graves as though I could find out who it was that had been sung so sweetly, and if it were man or woman. I've got it here," she said, taking a dainty ivory portemonnaie from her pocket, and picking out with two slim finger tips a folded slip of newspaper; "and I thought that maybe you might recognize the style of the writer, and perhaps know something of his history. For I believe he has one. There! that is only a part of the article of course, but it is the part that interested me. Just read from there," she pointed, leaning partly over his shoulder so that her soft breath stirred his hair, "to the end; it isn't long."

In the film that seemed to come across his eyes, suddenly the print appeared blurred and indistinct. But he knew that she had put into his hand something he had written after the death of his wife; something spontaneous and impulsive, when her loss still filled his days and nights and almost unconsciously swayed his pen. He remembered that his eyes had been as dim when he wrote it—and now—handed to him by this smiling, well-to-do woman, he was as shocked at first as if he had suddenly found her reading his private letters. This was followed by a sudden sense of shame that he had ever thus publicly bared his feelings, and then by the illogical but irresistible conviction that it was false and stupid. The few phrases she had pointed out appeared as cheap and hollow rhetoric amid the surroundings of their social tête-à-tête over the luncheon-table. There was small danger that this heady wine of woman's praise would make him betray himself; there was no sign of gratified authorship in his voice as he quietly laid down the paper and said drily: "I am afraid I can't help you. You know it may be purely fanciful."

"I don t think so," said Mrs. Ashwood thoughtfully. "At the same time it doesn't strike me as a very abiding grief for that very reason. It's too sympathetic. It strikes me that it might be the first grief of some one too young to be inured to sorrow or experienced enough to accept it as the common lot. But like all youthful impressions it is very sincere and true while it lasts. I don t know whether one gets anything more real when one gets older."

With an insincerity he could not account for, he now felt inclined to defend his previous sentiment, although all the while conscious of a certain charm in his companion's graceful scepticism. He had in his truthfulness and independence hitherto always been quite free from that feeble admiration of cynicism which attacks the intellectually weak and immature, and his present predilection may have been due more to her charming personality. She was not at all like his sisters; she had none of Clementina's cold abstraction, and none of Euphemia's sharp and demonstrative effusiveness. And in his secret consciousness of her nattering fore-knowledge. of him, with her assurance that before they had ever met he had unwittingly influenced her, he began to feel more at his ease. His fair companion also, in the equally secret knowledge she had acquired of his history, felt as secure as if she had been formally introduced. Nobody could find fault with her for showing civility to the ostensible son of her host—it was not necessary that she should be aware of their family differences. There was a charm too in their enforced isolation, in what was the exceptional solitude of the little hotel that day, and the seclusion of their table by the window of the dining-room, which gave a charming domesticity to their repast. From time to time they glanced down the lonely cañon, losing itself in the afternoon shadow. Nevertheless Mrs. Ashwood's pre-occupation with Nature did not preclude a human curiosity to hear something more of John Milton's quarrel with his father. There was certainly nothing of the prodigal son about him; there was no precocious evil knowledge in his frank eyes; no record of excesses in his healthy, fresh complexion; no unwholesome or disturbed tastes in what she had seen of his rural preferences and understanding of natural beauty. To have attempted any direct questioning that would have revealed his name and identity would have obliged her to speak of herself as his father's guest. She began indirectly; he had said he had been a reporter, and he was still a chronicler of this strange life. He had of course heard of many cases of family feuds and estrangements! Her brother had told her of some dreadful vendettas he had known in the south-west, and how whole families had been divided. Since she had been here she had heard of odd cases of brothers meeting accidentally after long and unaccounted separations; of husbands suddenly confronted with wives they had deserted; of fathers encountering discarded sons!

John Milton's face betrayed no- uneasy consciousness. If anything it was beginning to glow with a boyish admiration of the grace and intelligence of the fair speaker, that was perhaps heightened by an assumption of half coquettish discomfiture.

"You are laughing at me," she said finally. "But inhuman and selfish as these stories may seem, and sometimes are, I believe that these curious estrangements and separations often come from some fatal weakness of temperament that might be strengthened, or some trivial misunderstanding that could be explained. It is separation that makes them seem irrevocable only because they are inexplicable, and a vague memory always seems more terrible than a definite one. Facts may be forgiven and forgotten but mysteries haunt one always. I believe there are weak, sensitive people who dread, to put their wrongs into shape—those are the kind who sulk, and when you add separation to sulking, reconciliation becomes impossible. I knew a very singular case of that kind once. If you like, I'll tell it to you. Maybe you will be able, some day, to weave it into one of your writings. And it's quite true."

It is hardly necessary to say that John Milton had not been touched by any personal significance in his companion's speech, whatever she may have intended; and it is equally true that whether she had presently forgotten her purpose, or had become suddenly interested in her own conversation, her face grew more animated, her manner more confidential, and. something of the youthful enthusiasm she had shown in the mountain seemed to come back to her.

"I might say it happened anywhere and can the people M. or N., but it really did occur in my own family, and although I was much younger at the time it impressed me very strongly. My cousin, who had been my playmate, was an orphan, and had been entrusted to the care of my father, who was his guardian. He was always a clever boy, but singularly sensitive and quick to take offence. Perhaps it was because the little property his father had left made him partly dependent on my father, and that I was rich, but he seemed to feel the disparity in our positions. I was too young to understand it; I think it existed only in his imagination, for I believe we were treated alike. But I remember that he was full of vague threats of running away and going to sea, and that it was part of his weak temperament to terrify me with his extravagant confidences. I was always frightened when, after one of those scenes, he would pack his valise or perhaps only tie up a few things in a handkerchief, as in the advertisement pictures of the runaway slaves, and declare that we would never lay eyes upon him again. At first I never saw the ridiculousness of all this—for I ought to have told you that he was rather a delicate and timid boy, and quite unfitted for a rough life or any exposure—but others did, and one day I laughed at him and told him he was afraid. I shall never forget the expression of his face and never forgive myself for it. He went away,—but he returned the next day! He threatened once to commit suicide, left his clothes on the bank of the river, and came home in another suit of clothes he had taken with him. When I was sent abroad to school I lost sight of him; when I returned he was at college—apparently unchanged. When he came home for vacation,—far from having been subdued by contact with strangers—it seemed that his unhappy sensitiveness had been only intensified, by the ridicule of his fellows. He had even acquired a most ridiculous theory about the degrading effects of civilization, and wanted to go back to a state of barbarism. He said the wilderness was the only true home of man. My father, instead of bearing with what I believe was his infirmity, drily offered him the means to try his experiment. He started for some place in, Texas, saying we would never hear from him again. A month after he wrote for more money. My father replied rather impatiently?I suppose?I never knew exactly what he wrote. That was some years ago. He had told the truth at last, for we never heard from him again."

It is to be feared that John Milton was following the animated lips and eyes of the fair speaker rather than her story. Perhaps that was the reason why he said: "May he not have been a disappointed man?"

"I don t understand, she said simply.

"Perhaps," said John Milton with a boyish blush, "you may have unconsciously raised hopes in his heart—and?"

"I should hardly attempt to interest a chronicler of adventure like you in such a very commonplace, every-day style of romance," she said, with a little impatience, "even if my vanity compelled me to make such confidences to a stranger. No—t was nothing quite as vulgar as that. And," she added quickly, with a playfully amused smile as she saw the young fellow's evident distress, "I should have probably heard from him again. Those stories always end in that way."

"And you think??" said John Milton.

"I think," said Mrs. Ashwood slowly, "that he actually did commit suicide—or effaced himself in some way, just as firmly as I believe he might have been saved by judicious treatment. Otherwise we should have heard from him. You'll say that's only a woman's reasoning? but I think our perceptions are often instinctive, and I knew his character."

Still following the play of her delicate features into a romance of his own weaving, the imaginative young reporter, who had seen so much from the heights of Russian Hill, said earnestly: "Then I have your permission to use this material at any future time?"

"Yes," said the lady smilingly.

"And you will not mind if I should take some liberties with the text?"

"I must of course leave something to your artistic taste. But you will let me see it?"

There were voices outside now, breaking the silence of the verandah. They had been so preoccupied as not to notice the arrival of a horseman. Steps came along the passage; the landlord returned. Mrs. Ashwood turned quickly towards him.

"Mr. Grant, of your party, ma'am, to fetch you."

She saw an unmistakable change in her young friend's mobile face. "I will be ready in a moment," she said, to the landlord. Then turning to John Milton the arch-hypocrite said sweetly: "My brother must have known instinctively that I was in good hands as he didn't come. But I am sorry, for I should have so liked, to introduce him to you—although by the way," with a bright smile, "I don't think you have yet told me your name. I know I couldn't have forgotten it."

"Harcourt," said John Milton, with a half embarrassed laugh.

"But you must come and see me, Mr.—Mr. Harcourt," she said, producing a card from a case already in her fingers, "at my hotel, and let my brother thank you there for your kindness and gallantry to a stranger. I shall be here a few weeks longer before we go south to look for a place where my brother can winter. Do come and see me, although I cannot introduce you to anything as real and beautiful as what you have shown me to-day. Good-bye, Mr. Harcourt; I won t trouble you to come down and bore yourself with my escort's questions and congratulations."

She bent her head and allowed her soft eyes to rest upon his with a graciousness that was beyond her speech, pulled her veil over her eyes again, with a pretty suggestion that she had no further use for them, and taking her riding-skirt lightly in her hand seemed to glide from the room.

On her way to San Mateo, where it appeared the disorganized party had prolonged their visit to accept an invitation to dine with a local magnate, she was pleasantly conversational with the slightly abstracted Grant. She was so sorry to have given them all this trouble and anxiety! Of course she ought to have waited at the fork of the road, but she had never doubted but she could rejoin them presently on the main road. She was glad that Miss Euphemia's runaway horse had been stopped without accident; it would have been dreadful if anything had happened to her; Mr. Harcourt seemed so wrapped up in his girls. It was a pity they never had a son—Ah? Indeed! Then there was a son? So—and father and son had quarrelled? That was so sad. And for some trifling cause no doubt?

"I believe he married the housemaid," said Grant grimly. "Be careful!—Allow me."

"It's no use!" said Mrs. Ashwood, flushing with, pink impatience, as she recovered her seat which a sudden bolt of her mustang had imperiled. "I really can't make out the tricks of this beast! Thank you," she added, with a sweet smile, "but I think I can manage him now. I can t see why he stopped. I'll be more careful. You were saying the son was married—surely not that boy!"

"Boy!" echoed Grant. "Then you know—?"

"I mean of course he must be a boy—they all grew up here—and it was only five or six years ago that their parents emigrated," she retorted a little impatiently. And what about this creature?"

"Your horse?"

"You know I mean the woman he married. Of course she was older than he—and caught him?"

"I think there was a year or two difference," said Grant quietly.

"Yes, but your gallantry keeps you from telling the truth, which is that the women, in cases of this kind, are much older and more experienced."

"Are they? Well, perhaps she is now. She is dead."

Mrs. Ashwood walked her horse. "Poor thing," she said. Then a sudden idea took possession of her and brought a film to her eyes. "How long ago?" she asked in a low voice.

"About six or seven months, I think. I believe there was a baby who died too."

She continued to walk her horse slowly, stroking its curved neck. "I think it's perfectly shameful!" she said suddenly.

"Not so bad as that, Mrs. Ashwood, surely. The girl may have loved him—and he?"

"You know perfectly what I mean, Mr. Grant—I speak of the conduct of the mother and father and those two sisters!"

Grant slightly elevated his eyebrows. "But you forget, Mrs. Ashwood. It was young Harcourt and his wife's own act—they preferred to take their own path and keep it."

"I think," said Mrs. Ashwood authoritatively, "that the idea of leaving those two unfortunate children to suffer and. struggle on alone—out there—on the sand hills of San Francisco—was simply disgraceful!"

Later that evening she was unreasonably annoyed to find that her brother, Mr. John Shipley, had taken advantage of the absence of Grant to pay marked attention to Clementina, and had even prevailed upon that imperious goddess to accompany him after dinner on a moonlight stroll upon the verandah and terraces of Los Pajaros. Nevertheless she seemed to recover her spirits enough to talk volubly of the beautiful scenery she had discovered in her late perilous abandonment in the wilds of the Coast Range; to aver her intention to visit it again: to speak of it in a severely practical way as offering a far better site for the cottages of the young married couples just beginning life than the outskirts of towns or the bleak sand hills of San Francisco; and thence by graceful degrees into a dissertation upon popular fallacies in regard to hasty marriages, and the mistaken idea of some parents in not accepting the inevitable and making the best of it. She still found time to enter into an appreciative and exhaustive criticism upon the literature and journalistic enterprise of the Pacific Coast with the proprietor of the Pioneer, and to cause that gentleman to declare that whatever people might say about rich and fashionable Eastern women, that Mrs. Ashwood's head was about as level as it was pretty.

The next morning found her more thoughtful and subdued, and when her brother came upon her sitting on the verandah, while the party were preparing to return, she was reading a newspaper slip that she had taken from her porte-monnaie, with a face that was partly shadowed.

"What have you struck there, Conny?" said her brother gaily. "It looks too serious for a recipe."

"Something I should like you to read some time, Jack," she said, lifting her lashes with a slight timidity, "if you would take the trouble. I really wonder how it would impress you."

"Pass it over," said Jack Shipley good-humouredly, with his cigar between his lips. "I'll take it now."

She handed him the slip and turned partly away; he took it, glanced at it sideways, turned it over, and suddenly his look grew concentrated, and he took the cigar from his lips.

"Well," she said playfully, turning to him again. "What do you think of it?"

"Think of it?" he said with a rising colour. "I think it's infamous! Who did it?"

She stared at him, then glanced quickly at the slip. "What are you reading?" she said.

"This, of course," he said impatiently. "What you gave me." But he was pointing to the other side of the newspaper slip.

She took it from him impatiently and read for the first time the printing on the reverse side of the article she had treasured so long. It was the concluding paragraph of an apparently larger editorial. "One thing is certain, that a man in Daniel Harcourt's position cannot afford to pass over in silence accusations like the above, that affect not only his private character, but the integrity of his title to the land that was the foundation of his fortune. When trickery, sharp practice, and even criminality in the past are more than hinted at, they cannot be met by mere pompous silence or allusions to private position, social prestige, or distinguished friends in the present."

Mrs. Ashwood turned the slip over with scornful impatience, a pretty uplifting of her eyebrows and a slight curl of her lip. "I suppose none of those people's beginnings can bear looking into—and they certainly should be the last ones to find fault with anybody. But, good gracious, Jack! what has this to do with you?"

"With me?" said Shipley angrily. "Why I proposed to Clementina last night!"

CHAPTER IX

THE wayfarers on the Tasajara turnpike whom Mr. Daniel Harcourt passed with his fast trotting mare and sulky, saw that their great fellow-townsman was more than usually preoccupied and curt in his acknowledgment of their salutations. Nevertheless as he drew near the creek, he partly checked his horse, and when he reached a slight acclivity of the interminable plain—which had really been the bank of the creek in bygone days?he pulled up, alighted, tied his horse to a rail fence, and clambering over the enclosure made his way along the ridge. It was covered with nettles, thistles, and a few wiry dwarf larches of native growth; dust from the adjacent highway had invaded it with a few scattered and torn handbills, waste paper, rags, empty provision cans, and other suburban dèbris. Yet it was the site of Lige Curtis's cabin, long since erased and forgotten. The bed of the old creek had receded; the last tules had been cleared away; the channel and embarcadero were half a mile from the bank and log whereon the pioneer of Tasajara had idly sunned himself.

Mr. Harcourt walked on, occasionally turning over the scattered objects with his foot, and stopping at times to examine the ground more closely. It had not apparently been disturbed since he himself, six years ago, had razed the wretched shanty and carried off its timbers to aid in the erection of a larger cabin further inland. He raised his eyes to the prospect before him—to the town with its steamboats lying at the wharves, to the gram elevator, the warehouses, the railroad station with its puffing engines, the flagstaff of Harcourt House, and the clustering roofs of the town, and beyond the painted dome of his last creation, the Free Library. This was all his work, his planning, his foresight, whatever they might say of the wandering drunkard from whose tremulous fingers he had snatched the opportunity. They could not take that from him; however they might follow him with envy and reviling, any more than they could wrest from him the five years of peaceful possession. It was with something of the prosperous consciousness with which he had mounted the platform on the opening of the Free Library, that he now climbed into his buggy and drove away.

Nevertheless he stopped at his Land Office as he drove into town, and gave a few orders. "I want a strong picket fence put around the fifty vara lot in block fifty-seven, and the ground cleared up at once. Let me know when the men get to work and I'll overlook them."

Re-entering his own house in the square where Mrs. Harcourt and Clementina—who often accompanied him in those business visits—were waiting for him with luncheon, he smiled somewhat superciliously as the servant informed him that "Professor Grant had just arrived." Really that man was trying to make the most of his time with Clementina! Perhaps the rival attractions of that .Boston swell Shipley had something to do with it! He must positively talk to Clementina about this. In point of fact he himself was a little disappointed in Grant, who, since his offer to take the task of hunting down his calumniators, had really done nothing. He turned into his study, but was slightly astonished to find that Grant, instead of paying court to Clementina in the adjoining drawing-room, was sitting rather thoughtfully in his own armchair.

He rose as Harcourt entered. "I didn't let them announce me to the ladies," he said, "as I have some important business with you first, and we may find it necessary that I should take the next train back to town. You remember that a few weeks ago I offered to look into the matter of those slanders against you. I apprehended it would be a trifling matter of envy or jealousy on the part of your old associates or neighbours, which could be put straight with a little good feeling, but I must be frank with you, Harcourt, and say at the beginning that it turns out to be an infernally ugly business. Call it conspiracy if you like, or organized hostility, I'm afraid it will require a lawyer rather than an arbitrator to manage it, and the sooner the better. For the most unpleasant thing about it is, that I can't find out exactly how bad it is!"

Unfortunately the weaker instinct of Harcourt's nature was first roused; the vulgar rage which confounds the bearer of ill news with the news itself filled his breast. "And this is all that your confounded intermeddling came to?" he said brutally.

"No," said Grant quietly with a preoccupied ignoring of the insult that was more hopeless for Harcourt. "I found out that it is claimed that this Lige Curtis was not drowned nor lost that night; but that he escaped, and for three years has convinced another man that you are wrongfully in possession of this land; that these two naturally hold you in their power, and that they are only waiting for you to be forced into legal proceedings for slander to prove all their charges. Until then, for some reason best known to themselves, Curtis remains in the background."

"Does he deny the deed under which I hold the property?" said Harcourt savagely.

"He says it was only a security for a trifling loan, and not an actual transfer."

"And don t those fools know that his security could be forfeited?"

"Yes, but not in the way it is recorded in the County Clerk's office. They say that the record shows that there was an interpolation in the paper he left with you—which was a forgery. Briefly, Harcourt, you are accused of that. More—it is intimated that when he fell into the creek that night, and escaped on a raft that was floating past, that he had been first stunned by a blow from some one interested in getting rid of him."

He paused and glanced out of the window.

"Is that all?" asked Harcourt in a perfectly quiet, steady voice.

"All," replied Grant, struck with a change in his companion's manner and turning his eyes upon turn quickly.

The change indeed was marked and significant. Whether from relief at knowing the worst, or whether he was experiencing the same reaction from the utter falsity of this last accusation that he had felt when Grant had unintentionally wronged him in his previous recollection, certain it is that some unknown reserve of strength in his own nature, of which he knew nothing before, suddenly came to his aid in this extremity. It invested him with an uncouth dignity that for the first time excited Grant's respect.

"I beg your pardon, Grant, for the hasty way I spoke to you a moment ago, for I thank you, and appreciate thoroughly and sincerely what you have done. You are right; it is a matter for fighting, and not fussing over. But I must have a head to hit. Whose is it?"

"The man who holds himself legally responsible is Fletcher—the proprietor of the Clarion, and a man of property."

"The Clarion? That is the paper which began the attack?" said Harcourt.

"Yes, and it is only fair to tell you here that your son threw up his place on it in consequence of its attack upon you."

There was perhaps the slightest possible shrinking in Harcourt's eyelids—the one congenital likeness to his discarded son—but his otherwise calm demeanour did not change. Grant went on more cheerfully: "I've told you all I know. When I spoke of an unknown worst I did not refer to any further accusation but to whatever evidence they might have fabricated or suborned to prove any one of them. It is only the strength and fairness of the hands they hold that is uncertain. Against that you have your certain uncontested possession, the peculiar character and antecedents of this Lige Curtis which would make his evidence untrustworthy and even make it difficult for them to establish his identity. I am told that his failure to contest your appropriation of his property is explained by the fact of his being absent from the country most of the time; but again this would not account for their silence until within the last six months, unless they have been waiting for further evidence to establish it. But even then they must have known that the time of recovery had passed. You are a practical man, Harcourt, I needn't tell you therefore what your lawyer will probably tell you, that practically, so far as your rights are concerned, you remain as before these calumnies; that a cause of action unprosecuted or in abeyance is practically no cause, and that it is not for you to anticipate one. But —"

He paused and looked steadily at Harcourt. Harcourt met his look with a dull, ox-like stolidity. "I shall begin the suit at once," he said.

"And I," said Grant, holding out his hand, "will stand by you. But tell me now what you knew of this man Curtis—his character and disposition; it may be some clue as to what are his methods and his intentions."

Harcourt briefly sketched Lige Curtis as he knew him and understood him. It was another indication of his reserved power that the description was so singularly clear, practical, unprejudiced, and impartial that it impressed Grant with its truthfulness.

"I can't make him out," he said; "you have drawn a weak, but neither a dishonest nor malignant man. There must have been somebody behind him. Can you think of any personal enemy?"

"I have been subjected to the usual jealousy and envy of my old neighbours, I suppose, but nothing more. I have harmed no one knowingly."

Grant was silent; it had flashed across him that Rice might have harboured revenge for his father-in-law's interference in his brief matrimonial experience. He had also suddenly recalled his conversation with Billings on the day that he first arrived at Tasajara. It would not be strange if this man had some intimation of the secret. He would try to find him that evening. He rose.

"You will stay to dinner. My wife and Clementina will expect you."

"Not to-night; I am dining at the hotel," said Grant smilingly, "but I will come in later in the evening if I may." He paused hesitatingly for a moment. "Have your wife and daughter ever expressed any opinion on this matter?"

"No," said Harcourt. "Mrs. Harcourt knows nothing of anything that does not happen in the house; Euphemia knows only the things that happen out of it where she is visiting—and I suppose that young men prefer to talk to her about other things than the slanders of her father. And Clementina—well, you know how calm and superior to these things she is."

"For that very reason I thought that perhaps she might be able to see them more clearly—but no matter! I dare say you are quite right in not discussing them at home." This was the fact, although Grant had not forgotten that Harcourt had put forward his daughters as a reason for stopping the scandal some weeks before—a reason which however seemed never to have been borne out by any apparent sensitiveness of the girls themselves.

When Grant had left Harcourt remained for some moments steadfastly gazing from the window over the Tasajara plain. He had not lost his look of concentrated power, nor his determination to fight. A struggle between himself and the phantoms of the past had become now a necessary stimulus for its own sake—for the sake of his mental and physical equipoise. He saw before him the pale, agitated, irresolute features of Lige Curtis—not the man he had injured, but the man who had injured him, whose spirit was aimlessly and wantonly—for he had never attempted to get back his possessions in his lifetime, nor ever tried to communicate with the possessor—striking at him in the shadow. And it was that man, that pale, writhing, frightened wretch whom he had once mercifully helped! Yes, whose life he had even saved that night from, exposure and delirium, tremens when he had given him the whisky. And this life he had saved, only to have it set in motion a conspiracy to ruin him! Who knows that Lige had not purposely conceived what they had believed to be an attempt at suicide, only to cast suspicion of murder on him! From which it will be perceived that Harcourt's powers of moral reasoning had not improved in five years, and that even the impartiality he had just shown in his description of Lige to Grant had been swallowed up in this new sense of injury. The founder of Tasajara, whose cool business logic, unfailing foresight and practical deductions, were never at fault, was once more childishly adrift in his moral ethics.

And there was Clementina, of whose judgment Grant had spoken so persistently!—could she assist him? It was true, as he had said, he had never talked to her of his affairs; in his some-times uneasy consciousness of her superiority he had shrunk from even revealing his anxieties, much less his actual secret, and from anything that might prejudice the lofty paternal attitude he had taken towards his daughters from the beginning of his good fortune. He was never quite sure if her acceptance of it was real; he was never entirely free from certain jealousy that always mingled with his pride in her superior rectitude; and yet his feeling was distinct from the good-natured contempt he had for his wife's loyalty, the anger and suspicion that his son's opposition had provoked, and the half affectionate toleration he had felt for Euphemia's waywardness. However he would sound Clementina without betraying himself.

He was anticipated by a slight step in the passage and the pushing open of his study door.

The tall, graceful figure of the girl herself stood in the opening.

"They tell me Mr. Grant has been here. Does he stay to dinner?"

"No, he has an engagement at the hotel, but he will probably drop in later. Come in, Clemmy, I want to talk to you. Shut the door and sit down. "

She slipped in quietly, shut the door, took a seat on the sofa, softly smoothed down her gown, and turned her graceful head and serenely composed face towards him. Sitting thus she looked like some finely finished painting that decorated rather than belonged to the room—not only distinctly alien to the flesh and blood relative before her, but to the house, and even the local, monotonous landscape beyond the window with the shining new shingles and chimneys that cut the new blue sky. These singular perfections seemed to increase in Harcourt's mind, the exasperating sense of injury inflicted upon him by Lige's exposures. With a daughter so incomparably gifted—a matchless creation that was enough in herself to ennoble that fortune which his own skill and genius had lifted from the muddy tules of Tasajara where this Lige had left it—that she should be subjected to this annoyance seemed an infamy that Providence could not allow! What was his mere venial transgression to this exaggerated. retribution?

"Clemmy, girl, I'm going to ask you a question. Listen, Pet." He had begun with a reminiscent tenderness of the epoch of her child-hood, but meeting the unresponding maturity of her clear eyes he abandoned it. "You know, Clementina, I have never interfered in your affairs, nor tried to influence your friendships for anybody. Whatever people may have to say of me they can t say that! I've always trusted you, as I would myself, to choose your own associates; I have never regretted, it, and I don't regret it now. But I'd like to know—I have reasons to-day for asking—how matters stand between you and Grant."

The Parian head, of Minerva on the book-case above her did not offer the spectator a face less free from maidenly confusion than Clementina's at that moment. Her father had certainly expected none, but he was not prepared for the perfect coolness of her reply.

"Do yon mean have I accepted him?"

"No—well—yes."

"No, then! Is that what he wished to see you about? It was understood that he was not to allude again to the subject to any one."

"He has not to me. It was only my own idea. He had something very different to tell me. You may not know, Clementina," he began cautiously, "that I have been lately the subject of some anonymous slanders, and Grant has taken the trouble to track them down for me. It is a calumny that goes back as far as Sidon, and I may want your level head and good memory to help me to refute it." He then repeated calmly and clearly, with no trace of the fury that had raged within him a moment before, the substance of Grant's revelation.

The young girl listened without apparent emotion. When he had finished she said quickly: "And what do you want me to recollect?"

The hardest part of Harcourt's task was coming. "Well, don't you remember that I told you the day the surveyors went away—that—I had bought this land of Lige Curtis some time before?"

"Yes, I remember your saying so, but—"

"But what?"

"I thought you only -meant that to satisfy mother."

Daniel Harcourt felt the blood settling round his heart, but he was constrained, by an irresistible impulse to know the worst. "Well, what did you think, it really was?"

"I only thought that Lige Curtis had simply let you have it, that s all."

Harcourt breathed again. "But what for? Why should he?"

"Well— on my account"

"On your account! What in Heaven's name had you to do with it?"

"He loved me." There was not the slightest trace of vanity, self-consciousness or coquetry in her quiet fateful face, and for this very reason Harcourt knew that she was speaking the truth.

"Loved you! —you, Clementina !—my daughter! Did he ever tell you so?"

"Not in words. He used to walk up and down on the road when I was at the back window or in the garden, and often hung about the bank of the creek for hours, like some animal. I don t think the others saw him, and when they did they thought it was Parmlee for Euphemia. Even Euphemia thought so too, and that was why she was so conceited and hard to Parmlee towards the end. She thought it was Parmlee that night when Grant and Rice came; but it was Lige Curtis who had been watching the window lights in the rain, and who must have gone off at last to speak, to you in the store. I. always let Phemie believe that it was Parmlee—it seemed to please her."

There was not the least tone of mischief or superiority, or even of patronage in her manner. It was as quiet and cruel as the fate that might have led Lige to his destruction. Even her father felt a slight thrill of awe as she paused. "Then he never really spoke to you?" he asked hurriedly.

"Only once. I was gathering swamp lilies all alone, a mile below the bend of the creek, and he came upon me suddenly. Perhaps it was that I didn't jump or start— I didn't see anything to jump or start at—and. he said, 'You're not frightened at me, Miss Harcourt, like the other girls? You don't think I'm drunk or half mad—as they do?' I don't remember exactly what I said, but it meant that whether he was drunk or half mad or sober I didn't see any reason to be afraid of him. And then he told me that if I. was fond of swamp lilies I might have all I wanted at his place, and for the matter of that the place too, as he was going away, for he couldn't stand the loneliness any longer. He said that he had nothing in common with the place and the people—no more than I had—and that was what he had always fancied in me. I told him that if he felt in that way about his place he ought to leave it, or sell it to some one who cared for it, and. go away. That must have been in his mind when he offered it to you—at least that's what I thought when you told us you had bought it. I didn't know but what he might have told you—but you didn't care to say it before mother."

Mr. Harcourt sat gazing at her with breathless amazement. "And you—think that—Lige Curtis—lov—liked you?"

"Yes, I think he did—and that he does now!"

"Now! What do you mean? The man is dead!" said Harcourt starting.

"That s just what I don t believe."

"Impossible ! Think of what you are saying"

"I never could quite understand or feel that he was dead when everybody said so, and now that I've heard this story I know that he is living."

"But why did he not make himself known in time to claim the property?"

"Because he did not care for it."

"What did he care for, then?"

"Me, I suppose."

"But this calumny is not like a man who loves you."

"It is like a jealous one."

With an effort Harcourt threw on his bewildered incredulity and grasped the situation. He would have to contend with his enemy in the flesh and blood, but that flesh and blood would be very weak in the hands of the impassive girl beside him. His face lightened.

The same idea might have been in Clementina's mind when she spoke again, although her face had remained unchanged. "I do not see why you should bother yourself further about it, she said. "It is only a matter between myself and him; you can leave it to me."

"But if you are mistaken and he should not be living?"

"I am not mistaken. I am even certain now that I have seen him."

"Seen him!"

"Yes," said the girl with the first trace of animation in her face. "It was four or five months ago when we were visiting the Briones at Monterey. We had ridden out to the old Mission by moonlight. There were some Mexicans lounging around the posada, and one of them attracted my attention by the way he seemed to watch me, without revealing any more of his face than I could see between his serape and the black silk handkerchief that was tied around his head under his sombrero. But I knew he was an American—and his eyes were familiar. I believe it was he.

"Why did you not speak of it before?"

The look of animation died out of the girl's face. "Why should I?" she said listlessly. "I did not know of these -reports then. He was nothing more to us. You wouldn't have cared to see him again." She rose, smoothed out her skirt and stood looking at her father. "There is one thing of course that you will do at once."

Her voice had changed so oddly that lie said quickly: "What's that?"

"Call Grant off the scent. He'll only frighten or exasperate your game, and that's what you don t want."

Her voice was as imperious as it had been previously listless. And it was the first time he had ever known her to use slang. It seemed as startling as if it had fallen from the marble lips above him.

"But I've promised him that we should go together to my lawyer to-morrow, and begin a suit against the proprietors of the Clarion"

"Do nothing of the kind. Get rid of Grant's assistance in this matter; and see the Clarion proprietor yourself. What sort of a man is he? Can you invite him to your house?"

"I have never seen him; I believe he lives at San José. He is a wealthy man and a large landowner there. You understand that after the first article appeared in his paper, and I knew that he had employed your brother—although Grant says that he had nothing to do with it and left Fletcher on account of it—I could have no intercourse with him. Even if I invited him he would not come."

"He must come. Leave it to me ". She stopped and resumed her former impassive manner. "I had something to say to you too, father. Mr. Shipley proposed to me the day we went to San Mateo."

Her father's eyes lit with an eager sparkle. "Well," he said quickly.

"I reminded him that I had known him only a few weeks, and that I wanted time to consider."

"Consider! Why, Clemmy, he's one of the oldest Boston families, rich from his father and grandfather—rich when I was a shopkeeper and your mother—"

"I thought you liked Grant?" she said quietly.

"Yes, but if you have no choice nor feeling in the matter, why Shipley is far the better man. And if any of the scandal should come to his ears—"

"So much the better that the hesitation should come from me. But if you think it better, I can sit down here and write to him at once declining the offer." She moved towards the desk.

"No! No! I did not mean that, said Harcourt quickly. "I only thought that if he did hear anything it might be said that he had. backed out."

"His sister knows of his offer, and though she don't like it nor me she will not deny the fact. By the way, you remember when she was lost that day on the road to San Mateo?"

"Yes."

"Well, she was with your son, John Milton, all the time, and they lunched together at Crystal Spring. It came out quite accidentally through the hotel-keeper."

Harcourt s brow darkened. "Did she know him before?"

"I can't say; but she does now."

Harcourt's face was heavy with distrust. "Taking Shipley's offer and these scandals into consideration, I don't like the look of this, Clementina."

"I do," said the girl simply.

Harcourt gazed at her keenly and with the shadow of distrust still upon him. It seemed to be quite impossible, even with what he knew of her calmly cold nature, that she should be equally uninfluenced by Grant or Shipley. Had she some steadfast, lofty ideal—or perhaps some already absorbing passion of which he knew nothing? She was not a girl to betray it—they would only know it when it was too late. Could it be possible that there was still something between her and Lige, that he knew nothing of? The thought struck a chill to his breast. She was walking towards the door, when he recalled himself with an effort.

"If you think it advisable to see Fletcher, you might run down to San José for a day or two with your mother, and call on the Ramirez. They may know him or somebody who does. Of course if you meet him and casually invite him it would be different."

"It's a good idea," she said quickly. "I'll do it and speak to mother now."

He was struck by the change in her face and voice; they had both nervously lightened, as oddly and distinctly as they had before seemed to grow suddenly harsh and aggressive. She passed out of the room with girlish brusqueness, leaving him alone with a new and vague fear in his consciousness.

A few hours later Clementina was standing before the window of the drawing-room that overlooked the outskirts of the town. The moonlight was flooding the vast bluish Tasajara levels with a faint lustre, as if the waters of the creek had once more returned to them. In the shadow of the curtain beside her Grant was facing her with anxious eyes

"Then I must take this as your final answer, Clementina?"

"You must. And had I known of these calumnies before; had you been frank with me even the day we went to San Mateo, my answer would have been as final then, and you might have been spared any further suspense. I am not blaming you, Mr. Grant; I am willing to believe that you thought it best to conceal this from me—even at that time when you had just pledged yourself to find out its truth or falsehood—yet my answer would have been the same. So long as this stain rests on my father's name I shall never allow that name to be coupled with yours in marriage or engagement; nor will my pride or yours allow us to carry on a simple friendship after this. I thank you for your offer of assistance, but I cannot even accept that which might to others seem to allow some contingent claim. I. would rather believe that when you proposed this inquiry and my father permitted it, you both knew that it put an end to any other relations between us."

But, Clementina, you are wrong, believe me! Say that I have been foolish, indiscreet, mad—still the few who knew that I made these inquiries on your father's behalf know nothing of my hopes of you!"

"But I do, and that is enough for me."

Even in the hopeless preoccupation of his passion he suddenly looked at her with something of his old critical scrutiny. But she stood there calm, concentrated, self-possessed and upright. Yes! it was possible that the pride of this southwestern shopkeeper's daughter was greater than his own.

"Then you banish me, Clementina?"

"It is we whom you have banished."

"Good-night".

"Good-bye."

He bent for an instant over her cold hand and then passed out into the hall. She remained listening until the front door closed behind him. Then she ran swiftly through the hall and up the staircase with an alacrity that seemed impossible to the stately goddess of a moment before. When she had reached her bedroom and closed the door, so exuberant still and so uncontrollable was her levity and action, that without going round the bed which stood before her in the centre of the room, she placed her two hands upon it and lightly vaulted sideways across it to reach the window. There she watched the figure of Grant crossing the moonlit square. Then turning back into the half-lit room, she ran to the small dressing-glass placed at an angle on a toilet table against the wall. With her palms grasping her knees she stooped down suddenly and contemplated the mirror. It showed what no one but Clementina had ever seen—and she herself only at rare intervals—the laughing eyes and soul of a self-satisfied, material-minded, ordinary country girl.

CHAPTER X

BUT Mr. Lawrence Grant's character in certain circumstances would seem to have as startling and inexplicable contradictions as Clementina Harcourt's, and three days later he halted his horse at the entrance of .Los Gatos Rancho. The "Home of the Cats"—so called from the catamounts which infested the locality—which had for over a century lazily basked before one of the hottest cañons in the Coast Range, had lately been stirred into some activity by the American, Don Diego Fletcher, who had bought it, put up a saw-mill and deforested the cañon. Still there remained enough suggestion of a feline haunt about it to make Grant feel as if he had tracked hither some stealthy enemy, in spite of the peaceful intimation conveyed by the sign on a rough boarded shed at the wayside, that the "Los Gatos Land and Lumber Company" held their office there.

A cigarette-smoking peon lounged before the door. Yes; Don Diego was there, but as he had arrived from Santa Clara only last night and was going to Colonel Ramirez that afternoon, he was engaged. Unless the business was important—but the cool, determined manner of Grant, even more than his words, signified that it was important, and the servant led the way to Don Diego's presence.

There certainly was nothing in the appearance of this sylvan proprietor and newspaper capitalist to justify Grant's suspicion of a surreptitious foe. A handsome man scarcely older than himself, in spite of a wavy mass of perfectly white hair which contrasted singularly with his brown moustache and dark sunburned face. So disguising was the effect of these contradictions that he not only looked unlike anybody else, but even his nationality seemed to be a matter of doubt. Only his eyes, light blue and intelligent, which had a singular expression of gentleness and worry, appeared individual to the man. His manner was cultivated and easy. He motioned his visitor courteously to a chair.

"I was referred to you," said Grant almost abruptly, "as the person responsible for a series of slanderous attacks against Mr. Daniel Harcourt in the Clarion, of which paper I believe you are the proprietor. I was told that you declined to give the authority for your action, unless you were forced to by legal proceedings."

Fletcher's sensitive blue eyes rested upon Grant's with an expression of constrained pain and pity. "I heard of your inquiries, Mr. Grant; you were making them on behalf of this Mr. Harcourt or Harkutt"—he made the distinction with intentional deliberation—"with a view I believe to some arbitration. The case was stated to you fairly, I think; I believe I have nothing to add to it."

"That was your answer to the ambassador of Mr. Harcourt," said Grant coldly, "and as such I delivered it to him; but I am here to-day to speak on my own account."

What could be seen of Mr. Fletcher's lips appeared to curl in an odd smile. "Indeed, I thought it was—or would be—all in the family."

Grant's face grew more stern, and his grey eyes glittered. "You'll find my status in this matter so far independent that I don't propose, like Mr. Harcourt, either to begin a suit or to rest quietly under the calumny. Briefly, Mr. Fletcher, as you or your informant knows, I was the surveyor who revealed to Mr. Harcourt the value of the land to which he claimed a title from your man—this Elijah or Lige Curtis as you call him"—he could not resist this imitation of his adversary's supercilious affectation of precise nomenclature—"and it was upon my representation of its value as an investment that lie began the improvements which have made him wealthy. If this title was fraudulently obtained all the facts pertaining to it are sufficiently related to connect me with the conspiracy."

"Are you not a little hasty in your presumption, Mr. Grant?" said Fletcher, with unfeigned surprise.

"That is for me to judge, Mr. Fletcher," returned Grant haughtily.

"But the name of Professor Grant is known to all California as beyond the breath of calumny or suspicion."

"It is because of that fact that I propose to keep it so."

"And may I ask in what way you wish me to assist you in so doing?"

"By promptly and publicly retracting in the Clarion every word of this slander against Harcourt."

Fletcher looked steadfastly at the speaker. "And if I decline?"

"I think you have been long enough in California, Mr. Fletcher, to know the alternative expected of a gentleman," said Grant coldly.

Mr. Fletcher kept his gentle blue eyes—in which surprise still over-balanced their expression of pained concern—on Grant s face.

"But is this not more in the style of Colonel Starbottle than Professor Grant?" he asked with a faint smile.

Grant rose instantly with a white face. "You will have a better opportunity of judging," he said, "when Colonel Starbottle has the honour of waiting upon you from me. Meantime, I thank you for reminding me of the indiscretion into which my folly in still believing that this thing could be settled amicably, has led me."

He bowed coldly and withdrew. Nevertheless, as he mounted his horse and rode away, he felt his cheeks burning. Yet he had acted upon calm consideration; he knew that to the ordinary Californian experience there was nothing Quixotic nor exaggerated in the attitude he had taken. Men had quarrelled and fought on less grounds; he had even half convinced himself that he had been insulted, and that his own professional reputation demanded the withdrawal of the attack on Harcourt on purely business grounds; but he was not satisfied of the personal re-sponsibility of Fletcher nor of his gratuitous malignity. Nor did the man look like a tool in the hands of some unscrupulous and hidden enemy. However, he had played his card. If he succeeded only in provoking a duel with Fletcher, he at least would divert the public attention from Harcourt to himself. He knew that his superior position would throw the lesser victim in the background. He would make the sac-rifice; that was his duty as a gentleman, even if she would not care to accept it as an earnest of his unselfish love!

He had reached the point where the mountain track entered the Santa Clara turnpike when his attention was attracted by a handsome but old-fashioned carriage drawn by four white mules, which passed down the road before him and turned suddenly off into a private road. But it was not this picturesque gala equipage of some local Spanish grandee that brought a thrill to his nerves and a flash to his eye; it was the unmistakable, tall, elegant figure and handsome profile of Clementina, reclining in light gauzy wraps against the back seat! It was no fanciful resemblance, the outcome of his reverie—there never was any one like her!—it was she herself! But what was she doing here?

A vaquero cantered from the cross road where the dust of the vehicle still hung. Grant hailed him. Ah! it was a fine carroza, de cuatro mulas that he had just passed! Si, Señor, truly; it was of Don Jose Ramirez who lived just under the hill.

It was bringing company to the casa.

Ramirez! That was where Fletcher was going! Had Clementina known that he was one of Fletcher's friends? .Might she not be exposed to unpleasantness, marked coolness, or even insult in that unexpected meeting? Ought she not to be warned or prepared for it? She had banished Grant from her presence until this stain was removed from her father's name, but could she blame him for trying to save her from contact with her father's slanderer? No! he turned his horse abruptly into the cross road and spurred forward in the direction of the casa.

It was quite visible now—a low-walled, quadrangular mass of whitewashed adobe, lying like a drift on the green hillside. The carriage and four had far preceded him, and was already half up the winding road towards the house. Later he saw them reach the courtyard and disappear within. He would be quite in time to speak with her before she retired to change her dress. He would simply say that while making a professional visit to Los Gatos Land Company Office he had become aware of Fletcher's connection with it, and accidentally of his intended visit to Ramirez. His chance meeting with the carriage on the highway had determined his course.

As he rode into the courtyard he observed that it was also approached by another road, evidently nearer, Los Gatos, and probably the older and shorter communication between the two ranches. The fact was significantly demonstrated a moment later. He had given his horse to a servant, sent in his card to Clementina, and had dropped listlessly on one of the benches of the gallery surrounding the patio, when a horseman rode briskly into the opposite gateway, and dismounted with a familiar air. A waiting peon who recognized him, informed him that the Doña was engaged with a visitor, but that they were both returning to the gallery for chocolate in a moment. The stranger was the man he had left only an hour before— Don Diego Fletcher!

In an instant the idiotic fatuity of his position struck him fully. His only excuse for following Clementina had been to warn her of the coming of this man who had just entered, and who would now meet her as quickly as himself. For a brief moment the idea of quietly slipping out to the corral, mounting his horse again, and flying from the rancho, crossed his mind, but the thought that he would be running away from the man he had just challenged, and perhaps some new hostility that had sprung up in his heart against him, compelled him to remain. The eyes of both

men met; Fletcher's in half-wondering annoyance, Grant's in ill-concealed antagonism. What they would have said is not known, for at that moment the voice of
Clementina and Mrs. Ramirez were heard in the passage, and they both entered the
gallery. The two men were standing together; it was impossible to see one without
the other.

And yet Grant, whose eyes were instantly directed to Clementina, thought
that she had noted neither. She remained for an instant standing in the doorway in
the same self-possessed, coldly graceful pose he remembered she had taken on the
platform at Tasajara. Her eyelids were slightly downcast as if she had been arrested
by some sudden thought or some shy maiden sensitiveness; in her hesitation Mrs.
Ramirez passed impatiently before her.

"Mother of God!" said that lively lady, regarding the two speechless men, "is it
an indiscretion we are making here—or are you dumb? You, Don Diego, are loud
enough when you and Don José are together; at least introduce your friend."

Grant quickly recovered himself. "I am afraid," he said, coming forward, "unless Miss Harcourt does, that I am a mere trespasser in your house, señora. I saw her
pass in your carriage a few moments ago, and having a message for her I ventured
to follow her here."

"It is Mr. Grant, a friend of my father's," said Clementina, smiling with equa-
nimity as if just awakening from a momentary abstraction, yet apparently unconscious of Grant's imploring eyes, "but the other gentleman I have not the pleasure
of knowing."

"Ah—Don Diego Fletcher, a countryman of yours; and yet I think he knows
you not."

Clementina's face betrayed no indication of the presence of her father's foe,
and yet Grant knew that she must have recognized his name as she looked towards
Fletcher with perfect self-possession. He was too much engaged in watching her
to take note of Fletcher's manifest disturbance, or the evident effort with which
he at last bowed to her. That this unexpected double meeting with the daughter of
the man he had wronged, and the man who had espoused the quarrel, should be
confounding to him appeared only natural. But he was unprepared to understand
the feverish alacrity with which he accepted Doña Maria's invitation to chocolate,
or the equally animated way in which Clementina threw herself into her hostess's

Spanish levity. He knew it was an awkward situation that must be surmounted without a scene; he was quite prepared in the presence of Clementina to be civil to Fletcher, but it was odd that in this feverish exchange of courtesies and compliments, he, Grant, should feel the greater awkwardness, and be the most ill at ease. He sat down and took his part in the conversation; he let it transpire for Clementina's benefit, that he had been to Los Gatos only on business, yet there was no opportunity even for a significant glance, and he had the added embarrassment of seeing that she exhibited no surprise nor seemed to attach the least importance to his inopportune visit. In a miserable indecision he allowed himself to be carried away by the high-flown hospitality of his Spanish hostess, and consented to stay to an early dinner. It was part of the infelicity of circumstance that the voluble Doña Maria—electing him as the distinguished stranger above the resident Fletcher— monopolized him and attached him to her side. She would do the honours of her house; she must show him the ruins of the old Mission beside the corral; Don Diego and Clementina would join them presently in the garden. He cast a despairing glance at the placidly smiling Clementina, who was apparently equally indifferent to the evident constraint and assumed ease of the man beside her, and turned away with Mrs. Ramirez.

A silence fell upon the gallery so deep that the receding voices and footsteps of Grant and his hostess in the long passage were distinctly heard until they reached the end. Then Fletcher arose with an inarticulate exclamation! Clementina instantly put her finger to her lips, glanced around the gallery, extended her hand to him and saying "Come," half-led, half-dragged him into the passage. To the right she turned and pushed open the door of a small room that seemed a combination of boudoir and oratory, lit by a French window opening to the garden, and flanked by a large black and white crucifix with a prie Dicu beneath it. Closing the door behind them she turned and faced her companion. But it was no longer the face of the woman who had been sitting in the gallery, it was the face that had looked back at her from the mirror at Tasajara the night that Grant had left her—eager, flushed, material with common place excitement!

"Lige Curtis," she said.

"Yes," he answered passionately, "Lige Curtis, whom you thought dead! Lige Curtis, whom you once pitied, condoled with and despised! Lige Curtis! whose lands and property have enriched you ! Lige Curtis! who would have shared it with you freely at the time, but whom your father juggled and defrauded of it! Lige Curtis, branded by him as a drunken outcast and suicide ! Lige Curtis—"

"Hush!" She clapped her little hand over his mouth with a quick but awkward schoolgirl gesture—inconceivable to any who had known her usual languid elegance of motion—and held it there. He struggled angrily, impatiently, reproachfully, and then with a sudden characteristic weakness that seemed as much of a revelation as her once hoydenish manner—kissed it, when she let it drop. Then placing both her hands still girlishly on her slim waist and curtseying grotesquely before him, she said—

"Lige Curtis ! Oh yes! Lige Curtis who swore to do everything for me! Lige Curtis, who promised to give up liquor for me who was to leave Tasajara for me! Lige Curtis who was to reform, and keep his land as a nest egg for us both in the future, and then who sold it—and himself—and me—to dad for a glass of whisky! Lige Curtis who disappeared, and then let us think he was dead only that he might attack us out of the ambush of his grave!"

"Yes, but think what I have suffered all these years—not for the cursed land— you know I. never cared for that—but for you —you, Clementina— you rich, admired by every one: idolized, held far above me— me, the forgotten outcast, the wretched suicide—and yet the man to whom you had once plighted your troth. Which of those greedy fortune-hunters whom my money—my life-blood as you might have thought it was—attracted to you, did you care to tell that you had ever slipped out of the little garden gate at Sidon to meet that outcast! Do you wonder that as the years passed and you were happy, I did not choose to be so forgotten? Do you wonder that when you shut the door on the past I managed to open it again—if only a little way—that its light might startle you?"

Yet she did not seem startled or disturbed, and remained only looking at him critically.

"You say that you have suffered," she replied with a smile. "You don't look it! Your hair is white, but it is becoming to you, and you are a handsomer man, Lige Curtis, than you were when I first met you; you are finer," she went on still regarding him, "stronger and healthier than you were five years ago; you are rich and prosperous, you have everything to make you happy, but—"—here she laughed a little, held out both her hands, taking his and holding his arms apart in a rustic, homely fashion—"but you are still the same old Lige Curtis! It was like you to go off and hide yourself in that idiotic way; it was like you to let the property slide in that stupid, unselfish fashion; it was like you to get real mad, and say all those mean, silly things to dad, that didn't hurt him—in your regular looney style—for rich or poor, drunk or sober, ragged or elegant, plain or handsome—you're always the same -Lige Curtis!"

In proportion as that material, practical, rustic self—which nobody but Lige Curtis had ever seen—came back to her, so in proportion the irresolute, wavering, weak and emotional vagabond of Sidon came out to meet it. He looked at her with a vague smile, his five years of childish resentment, albeit carried on the shoulders of a man mentally and morally her superior, melted away. He drew her towards him, yet at the same moment a quick suspicion returned.

"Well, and what are you doing here? Has this man who has followed you any right, any claim upon you?"

"None but what you in your folly have forced upon him! You have made him father's ally. I don't know why he came here. I only know why I did—to find you!"

"You suspected then?"

"I knew! Hush!"

The returning voices of Grant and of Mrs. Ramirez were heard in the court-yard. Clementina made a warning yet girlishly mirthful gesture, again caught his hand, drew him quickly to the French window, slipped through it with him into the garden, where they were quickly lost in the shadows of a ceanothus hedge.

"They have probably met Don José in the orchard, and as he and Don Diego have business together, Doña Clementina has without doubt gone to her room and left them. For you are not very entertaining to the ladies to-day—you two caballeros! You have much politics together, eh?—or you have discussed and disagreed, eh? I will look for the senorita, and let you go, Don Distraido!"

It is to be feard that Grant's apologies and attempts to detain her were equally feeble—as it seemed to him that this was the only chance he might have of seeing her except in company with Fletcher. As Mrs. Ramirez left he lit a cigarette and listlessly walked up and down the gallery. But Clementina did not come—neither did his hostess return. A subdued step in the passage raised his hopes—it was only the grizzled major domo, to show him his room that he might prepare for dinner.

He followed mechanically down the long passage to a second corridor. There was a chance that he might meet Clementina, but he reached his room without encountering any one. It was a large vaulted apartment with a single window, a deep embrasure in the thick wall that seemed to focus like a telescope some forgotten sequestered part of the leafy garden. While washing his hands, gazing absently at the green vignette framed by the dark opening, his attention was drawn to a movement of the foliage, stirred apparently by the rapid passage of two half-hidden figures. The quick flash of a feminine skirt seemed to indicate the coy flight of some romping maid of the casa, and the pursuit and struggle of her vaquero swain. To a despairing lover even the spectacle of innocent, pastoral happiness in others is not apt to be soothing, and Grant was turning impatiently away when he suddenly stopped with a rigid face and quickly approached the window. In her struggles with the unseen Corydon, the clustering leaves seemed to have yielded at the same moment with the coy Chloris, and parting—disclosed a stolen kiss! (Grant's hand lay like ice against the wall. For, disengaging Fletcher's arm from her waist and freeing her skirt from the foliage, it was the calm, passionless Clementina herself who stepped out, and moved pensively towards the casa.

CHAPTER XI

"READERS of the Clarion will have noticed that allusion has been frequently made in these columns to certain rumours concerning the early history of Tasajara which were supposed to affect the pioneer record of .Daniel Harcourt. It was deemed by the conductors of this journal to be only consistent with the fearless and independent duty undertaken by the Clarion that these rumours should be fully chronicled as part of the information required by the readers of a first-class newspaper, unbiassed, by any consideration of the social position of the parties, but simply as a matter of news. For this the Clarion does not deem it necessary to utter a word of apology. But for that editorial comment or attitude which the proprietors felt was justified by the reliable sources of their information they now consider it only due in honour to themselves, their readers, and Mr. Harcourt to fully and freely apologize. A patient and laborious investigation enables them to state that the alleged facts published by the Clarion and copied by other journals are utterly unsupported by testimony, and. the charges—although more or less vague—which were based upon them are equally untenable. We are now satisfied that one 'Elijah Curtis' a former pioneer of Tasajara who disappeared five years ago, and was supposed to be drowned, has not only made no claim to the Tasajara property, as alleged, but has given no sign of his equally alleged. resuscitation and present existence, and that on the minutest investigation there appears nothing either in his disappearance, or the transfer of his property to Daniel Harcourt, that could in any way disturb the uncontested title to Tasajara or the unimpeachable character of its present owner. The whole story now seems to have been the outcome of one of those stupid rural hoaxes too common in California."

"Well," said Mrs. Ashwood laying aside the Clarion with a sceptical shrug of her pretty shoulders, as she glanced up at her brother. "I suppose this means that you are going to propose again to the young lady?"

"I have," said Jack Shipley; "that's the worst of it—and got my .answer before this came out."

"Jack!" said Mrs. Ashwood, thoroughly surprised.

"Yes ! You see, Conny, as I told you three weeks ago, she said she wanted time to consider—that she scarcely knew me, and all that! Well, I thought it wasn't ex-actly a gentleman's business to seem to stand off after that last attack on her father, and so, last week, I went down to San José where she was staying and begged her not to keep me in suspense. And, by Jove! she froze me with a look, and said that with these aspersions on her father's character, she preferred not to be under obli-gations to any one."

"And you believed her?"

"Oh hang it all! Look here, Conny—I wish you'd just try for once to find out some good in that family, besides what that sentimental young widower John Mil-ton may have. You seem to think because they've quarrelled with him there isn't a virtue left among them."

Far from seeming to offer any suggestion of feminine retaliation, Mrs. Ash-wood smiled sweetly. "My dear Jack, I have no desire to keep you from trying your luck again with Miss Clementina, if that's what you mean, and indeed I shouldn't be surprised if a family who felt a mésalliance as sensitively as the Harcourts felt that affair of their son's, would be as keenly alive to the advantages of a good match for their daughter. As to young Mr. Harcourt, he never talked to me of the vices of his family, nor has he lately troubled me much with the presence of his own virtues. I haven t heard from him since we came here.

"I suppose he is satisfied with the Government berth you got for him," returned, her brother drily.

"He was very grateful to Senator Flynn, who appreciates his talents,—but who offered it to him as a mere question of fitness," replied Mrs. Ashwood with great precision of statement. "But you don't seem to know he declined, it on account of his other work."

"Preferred his old Bohemian ways, eh? You can't change those fellows, Conny. They can't get over the fascinations of vagabondage. Sorry your lady-patroness scheme didn't work. Pity you couldn't have promoted him in the line of his profession, as the Grand Duchess of Girolstein did Fritz."

"For Heaven's sake, Jack, go to Clementina! You may not be successful, but there at least the perfect gentlemanliness and good taste of your illustrations will not be thrown away."

"I think of going to San Francisco to-morrow anyway," returned Jack with affected carelessness. "I'm getting rather bored with this wild seaside watering-place and its glitter of ocean and hopeless background of mountain. Its nothing to me that 'there's no land nearer than Japan' out there. It may be very healthful to the. tissues but it's weariness to the spirit, and I don't see why we can't wait at San .Francisco till the rains send us further south, as well as here."

He had walked to the balcony of their sitting-room in the little seaside hotel where this conversation took place, and gazed discontentedly over the curving bay and sandy shore before him. After a slight pause Mrs. Ashwood stepped out beside him.

"Very likely I may go with you," she said with a perceptible tone of weariness. "We will see after the post arrives."

"By the way, there is a little package for you in my room that came this morning. I brought it up, but forgot to give it you. You'll find it on my table."

Mrs. Ashwood abstractedly turned away and entered her brother's room from the same balcony. The forgotten parcel, which looked like a roll of manuscript, was lying on his dressing-table. She gazed attentively at the handwriting on the wrapper and then gave a quick glance around her. A sudden and subtle change came over her. She neither flushed nor paled, nor did the delicate lines of expression in her face quiver or change. But as she held the parcel in her hand her whole being seemed to undergo some exquisite suffusion. As the medicines which the Arabian physician had concealed in the hollow handle of the mallet permeated the languid royal blood of Persia, so some volatile balm of youth seemed to flow in upon her with the contact of that strange missive and transform her weary spirit.

"Jack!" she called in a high clear voice.

But Jack had already gone from the balcony when she reached it with an elastic step and a quick youthful swirl and rustling of her skirt. He was lighting his cigar in the garden.

"Jack," she said, leaning half over the railing; "come back here in an hour and we'll talk over that matter of yours again."

Jack looked up eagerly and as if he might even come up then, but she added quickly, "In about an hour—I must think it over," and withdrew.

She re-entered the sitting-room, shut the door carefully and locked it, half pulled down the blind, walking once or twice around the table on which the parcel lay, with one eye on it like a graceful cat. Then she suddenly sat down, took it up with a grave, practical face, examined the postmark curiously, and opened it with severe deliberation. It contained a manuscript and a letter of four closely written pages. She glanced at the manuscript with bright approving eyes, ran her fingers through its leaves and then laid it carefully and somewhat ostentatiously on the table beside her. Then, still holding the letter in her hand, she rose and glanced out of the window at her bored brother lounging towards the beach and at the heaving billows beyond, and returned to her seat. This apparently important preliminary concluded, she began to read.

There were, as already stated, four blessed pages of it! All vital, earnest, palpitating with youthful energy preposterous in premises, precipitate in conclusions— yet irresistible and convincing to every woman in their illogical sincerity. There was not a word of love in it, yet every page breathed a wholesome adoration; there was not an epithet or expression mat a greater prude than Mrs. .Ashwood would have objected to, yet every sentence seemed to end in a caress. There was not a line of poetry in it, and scarcely a figure or simile, and yet it was poetical. Boyishly egotistic as it was in attitude, it seemed to be written less of himself than to her; in its delicate because unconscious flattery, it made her at once the provocation and excuse. And yet so potent was its individuality that it required no signature. No one but John Milton Harcourt could have written it. His personality stood out of it so strongly that once or twice Mrs. Ashwood almost unconsciously put up her little hand before her face with a half mischievous, half deprecating smile, as if the big honest eyes of its writer were upon her.

It began by an elaborate apology for declining the appointment offered him by one of her friends, which he was bold enough to think had been prompted by her kind heart. That was like her, but yet what she might do to any one; and he preferred to think of her as the sweet and gentle lady who had recognized his merit without knowing him, rather than the powerful and gracious benefactress who wanted to reward him when she did know him. The crown that she had all unconsciously placed upon his head that afternoon at the little hotel at Crystal Spring was more to him than the Senator's appointment; perhaps he was selfish, but he could not bear that she who had given so much should believe that he could accept a lesser gift. All this and much more! Some of it he had wanted to say to her in San Francisco at times when they had met, but he could not find the words. But she had given him the courage to go on and do the only thing he was fit for, and he had resolved to stick to that, and perhaps do something once more that might make him hear again her voice as he had heard it that day, and again see the light that had shone in her eyes as she sat there and read. And this was why he was sending her a manuscript. She might have forgotten that she had told him a strange story of her cousin who had disappeared—which she thought he might at some time work up. Here it was. Perhaps she might not recognize it again in the way he had written it here; perhaps she did not really mean it when she had given him permission to use it—but he remembered her truthful eyes and believed her—and in any event it was hers to do with what she liked. It had been a great pleasure for him to write it and think that she would see it; it was like seeing her himself—that was in his better self —more worthy the companionship of a beautiful and noble woman than the poor young man she would have helped. This was why he had not called the week before she went away. But for all that, she had made his life less lonely, and he should be ever grateful to her. He could never forget how she unconsciously sympathized with him that day over the loss that had blighted his life for ever,—yet even then he did not know that she, herself, had passed through the same suffering. But just here the stricken widow of thirty, after a vain attempt to keep up the knitted gravity of her eyebrows, bowed her dimpling face over the letter of the blighted widower of twenty, and laughed so long and silently that the tears stood out like dew on her light-brown eyelashes.

But she became presently severe again, and finished her reading of the letter gravely. Then she folded it carefully, deposited it in a box on her table which she locked. After a few minutes, however, she unlocked the box again and transferred the letter to her pocket. The serenity of her features did not relax again although her previous pretty prepossession of youthful spirit was still indicated in her movements. Going into her bedroom, she reappeared in a few minutes, with a light cloak thrown over her shoulders and a white-trimmed, broad-brimmed hat. Then she rolled up the manuscript in a paper, and called her French maid. As she stood there awaiting her with the roll in her hand, she might have been some young girl on her way to her music lesson.

"If my brother returns before I do tell him to wait."

"Madame is going—"

"Out," said Mrs. Ashwood blithely, and tripped down stairs.

She made her way directly to the shore where she remembered there was a group of rocks affording a shelter from the north-west trade winds. It was reached at low water by a narrow ridge of sand, and here she had often basked in the sun with her book. It was here that she now unrolled John Milton's manuscript and read.

It was the story she had told him, but interpreted by his poetry and adorned by his fancy until the facts as she remembered them seemed to be no longer hers, or indeed truths at all. She had always believed her cousin's unhappy temperament to have been the result of a moral and physical idiosyncrasy—she found them here to be the effect of a lifelong and hopeless passion for herself! The ingenious John Milton had given a poet's precocity to the youth whom she had only known as a suspicious, moody boy, had idealized him as a sensitive but songless Byron, had given him the added infirmity of pulmonary weakness, and a handkerchief that in moments of great excitement, after having been hurriedly pressed to his pale lips, was withdrawn "with a crimson stain.". Opposed to this interesting figure—the more striking to her as she had been hitherto haunted by the impression that her cousin during his boyhood had been subject to facial eruption and boils—was her own equally idealized self. Cruelly kind to her cousin and gentle with his weaknesses while calmly ignoring their cause, leading him unconsciously step by step in his fatal passion, he only became aware by accident that she nourished an ideal hero in the person of a hard, proud, middle-aged, practical man of the world—her future husband ! At this picture of the late Mr. Ashwood, who had really been an indistinctive social bon vivant, his amiable relict grew somewhat hysterical. The discovery of her real feelings drove the consumptive cousin into a secret, self-imposed exile on the shores of the Pacific, where he hoped to find a grave. But the complete and sudden change of life and scene, the balm of the wild woods and the wholesome barbarism of nature, wrought a magical change in his physical health and a philosophical rest in his mind. He married the daughter of an Indian chief. Years passed, the heroine—a rich and still young and beautiful widow—unwittingly sought the same medicinal solitude. Here in the depths of the forest she encountered her former playmate; the passion which he had fondly supposed was dead, revived in her presence, and for the first time she learned from his bearded lips the secret of his passion. Alas! not she alone! The contiguous forest could not be bolted out, and the Indian wife heard all. Recognizing the situation with aboriginal directness of purpose, she committed suicide in the fond belief that it would reunite the survivors. But in vain, the cousins parted on the spot to meet no more.

Even Mrs. Ashwood's predilection for the youthful writer could not overlook the fact that the dénoûment was by no means novel nor the situation human, but yet it was here that she was most interested and fascinated. The description of the forest was a description of the wood where she had first met Harcourt; the charm of it returned, until she almost seemed to again inhale its balsamic freshness in the pages before her. Now, as then, her youth came back with the same longing and regret. But more bewildering than all, it was herself that moved there, painted with the loving hand of the narrator. For the first time she experienced the delicious flattery of seeing herself as only a lover could see her. The smallest detail of her costume was suggested with an accuracy that pleasantly thrilled her feminine sense. The grace of her figure slowly moving through the shadow, the curves of her arm and the delicacy of her hand that held the bridle rein, the gentle glow of her softly rounded cheek, the sweet mystery of her veiled eyes and forehead, and the escaping gold of her lovely hair beneath her hat were all in turn masterfully touched or tenderly suggested. And when to this was added the faint perfume of her nearer presence—the scent she always used—the delicate revelations of her withdrawn gauntlet, the bracelet clasping her white wrist, and at last the thrilling contact of her soft hand on his arm—she put down the manuscript and blushed like a very girl. Then she started.

A shout!— his voice surely!—and the sound of oars in their rowlocks.

An instant revulsion of feeling overtook her. With a quick movement she instantly hid the manuscript beneath her cloak and stood up erect and indignant. Not twenty yards away, apparently advancing from the opposite shore of the bay, was a boat. It contained only John Milton resting on his oars and scanning the group of rocks anxiously. His face, which was quite strained with anxiety, suddenly flushed when he saw her, and then recognizing the unmistakable significance of her look and attitude, paled once more. He bent over his oars again: a few strokes brought him close to the rock.

"I beg your pardon," he said hesitatingly, as he turned towards her and laid aside his oars, "but I thought you were—in danger."

She glanced quickly round her. She had forgotten the tide! The ledge between her and the shore was already a foot under brown sea-water. Yet if she had not thought that it would have looked ridiculous she would have leaped down even then and waded ashore.

"It's nothing," she said coldly, with the air of one to whom the situation was an everyday occurrence, "it's only a few steps and a slight wetting—and my brother would have been here in a moment more."

John Milton's frank eyes made no secret of his mortification. "I ought not to have disturbed you, I know," he said quickly; "I had no right. But I was on the other shore opposite and I saw you come down here—that is—"—he blushed prodigiously—"I thought it might be you—and I ventured—I—mean—won't you let me row you ashore?"

There seemed to be no reasonable excuse for refusing. She slipped quickly into the boat without waiting for his helping hand, avoiding that contact which only a moment ago she was trying to recall.

A few strokes brought them ashore. He continued his explanation with the hopeless frankness and persistency of youth and inexperience. "I only came here the day before yesterday. I would not have come, but Mr. Fletcher, who has a cottage or the other shore, sent for me to offer me my old place on the Clarion. I had no idea of intruding upon your privacy by calling here without permission."

Mrs. Ashwood had resumed her conventional courtesy without however losing her feminine desire to make her companion pay for the agitation he had caused her. "We would have been always pleased to see you," she said vaguely, "and I hope, as you are here now, you will come with me to the hotel. My brother—"

But he still retained his hold of the boat rope without moving, and continued:

"I saw you yesterday, through the telescope, sitting in your balcony; and later at night I think it was your shadow I saw near the blue shaded lamp in the sitting-room by the window—I don't mean the red lamp that you have in your own room. I watched you until you put out the blue lamp and lit the red one. I tell you this—because—because—I thought you might be reacting a manuscript I sent you. At least," he smiled faintly, "I liked to think it so."

In her present mood this struck her only as persistent and somewhat egotistical. But she felt herself now on ground where she could deal firmly with him.

"Oh, yes," she said gravely. "I got it and thank you very much for it. I intended to write to you."

"Don't," he said, looking at her fixedly, "I can see you don't like it."

"On the contrary," she said promptly, "I think it beautifully written, and very ingenious in plot and situation. Of course it isn't the story I told you—I didn't expect that, for I'm not a genius. The man is not at all like my cousin, you know, and the woman—well, really, to tell the truth, she is simply inconceivable!"

"You think so?" he said gravely. He had been gazing abstractedly at some shining brown sea-weed in the water and when he raised his eyes to hers they seemed to have caught its colour.

"Think so? I'm positive! There's no such a woman, she isn't human. But let us walk to the hotel."

"Thank you, but I must go back now."

"But at least let my brother thank you for taking his place—in rescuing me. It was so thoughtful in you to put off at once when you saw I was surrounded. I might have been in great danger."

"Please don't make fun of me, .Mrs. Ashwood," he said with a faint return of his boyish smile. "You know there was no danger. I have only interrupted you in a nap or a reverie—and I can see now that you evidently came here to be alone."

Holding the manuscript more closely hidden under the folds of her cloak, she smiled enigmatically. "I think I did, and it seems that the tide thought so too, and acted upon it. But you will come up to the hotel with me surely?"

"No, I am going back now." There was a sudden firmness about the young fellow which she had never before noticed. This was evidently the creature who had married in spite of his family.

"Won't you come back long enough to take your manuscript? I will point out the part I refer to and—we will talk it over."

"There is no necessity. I wrote to you that you might keep it; it is yours; it was written for you and none other. It is quite enough for me to know that you were good enough to read it. But will you do one thing more for me? Read it again! If you find anything in it the second time to change your views—if you find—"

"I will let you know," she said quickly. "I will write to you as I intended."

"No, I didn't mean that. I meant that if you found the woman less inconceivable and more human, don't write to me but put your red lamp in your window instead of the blue one. I will watch for it and see it."

"I think I shall be able to explain myself much better with simple pen and ink," she said drily, "and it will be much more useful to you."

He lifted his hat gravely, shoved off the boat, leaped into it, and before she could hold out her hand was twenty feet away. She turned and ran quickly up the rocks. When she reached the hotel, she could see the boat already half across the bay.

Entering her sitting-room she found that her brother, tired of waiting for her, had driven out. Taking the hidden manuscript from her cloak she tossed it with a slight gesture of impatience on the table. Then she summoned the landlord.

"Is there a town across the bay?"

"No! the whole mountain-side belongs to Don Diego Fletcher. He lives away back in the coast range, at Los Gatos, but he has a cottage and mill on the beach."

"Don Diego Fletcher—Fletcher! Is he a Spaniard then?"

"Half and half I reckon; he's from the lower country, I believe."

"Is he here often?"

"Not much; he has mills at Los Gatos, wheat-ranches at Santa Clara, and owns a newspaper in 'Frisco! But he's here now. There were lights in his house last night, and his cutter lies off the point."

"Could you get a small package and note to him?"

"Certainly; it is only a row across the bay."

"Thank you."

Without removing her hat and cloak she sat down at the table and began a letter to Don Diego Fletcher. She begged to enclose to him a manuscript which she was satisfied, for the interests of its author, was better in his hands than hers. It had been given to her by the author, Mr. J. M. Harcourt, whom she understood was engaged on Mr. Fletcher's paper, the Clarion, In fact, it had been written at her suggestion, and from an incident in real life of which she was cognizant. She was sorry to say that on account of some very foolish criticism of her own as to the facts, the talented young author had become so dissatisfied with it as to make it possible that, if left to himself, this very charming and beautifully written story would remain unpublished. As an admirer of Mr. Harcourt's genius, and a friend of his family, she felt that such an event would be deplorable, and she therefore begged to leave it to Mr. Fletcher's delicacy and tact to arrange with the author for its publication. She knew that Mr. Fletcher had only to read it to be convinced of its remarkable literary merit, and she again would impress upon him the fact that her playful and thoughtless criticism—which was personal and confidential—was only based upon the circumstances that the author had really made a more beautiful and touching story than the poor facts which she had furnished seemed to warrant. She had only just learnt the fortunate circumstance that Mr. Fletcher was in the neighbourhood of the hotel where she was staying with her brother.

With the same practical, business-like directness, but perhaps a certain unbusiness-like haste superadded, she rolled up the manuscript and despatched it with the letter.

This done, however, a slight reaction set in, and having taken off her hat and shawl, she dropped listlessly on a chair by the window, but as suddenly rose and took a seat in the darker part of the room. She felt that she had done right—that highest but most depressing of human convictions! It was entirely for his good. There was no reason why his best interests should suffer for his folly. If anybody was to suffer it was she. .But what nonsense was she thinking! She would write to him, later when she was a little cooler—as she had said. But then he had distinctly told her, and very rudely too, that he didn't want her to write. Wanted her to make signals to him—the idiot! and probably was even now watching her with a telescope. It was really too preposterous!

The result was that her brother found her on his return in a somewhat uncertain mood, and, as a counsellor, variable and conflicting in judgment. If this Clementina, who seemed to have the family qualities of obstinacy and audacity, really cared for him, she certainly wouldn't let delicacy stand in the way of letting him know it—and he was therefore safe to wait a little. A few moments later, she languidly declared that she was afraid that she was no counsellor in such matters; really she was getting too old to take any interest in that sort of thing, and she never had been a match-maker! By the way now, wasn't it odd that this neighbour, that rich capitalist across the bay, should be called Fletcher, and "James Fletcher" too, for Diego meant "James" in Spanish. Exactly the same name as poor Cousin Jim who disappeared. Did he remember her old playmate Jim? But her brother thought something else was a deuced sight more odd, namely, that this same Don Diego Fletcher was said to be very sweet on Clementina now, and was always in her company at the Ramirezes. And that, with this Clarion apology on the top of it, looked infernally queer.

Mrs. Ashwood felt a sudden consternation. Here had she—Jack's sister—just been taking Jack's probable rival into confidential correspondence! She turned upon Jack sharply:

"Why didn't you say that before?"

"I did tell you," he said gloomily, "but you didn't listen. But what difference does it make to you now?"

"None whatever," said Mrs. Ashwood calmly as she walked out of the room.

Nevertheless the afternoon passed wearily, and her usual ride into the upland cañon did not reanimate her. For reasons known best to herself she did not take her after dinner stroll along the shore to watch the outlying fog. At a comparatively early hour, while there was still a roseate glow in the western sky, she appeared with grim deliberation, and the blue lamp shade in her hand, and placed it over the lamp which she lit and stood on her table beside the window. This done she sat down and began to write with bright-eyed but vicious complacency.

"But you don't want that light and the window, Constance," said Jack wonderingly.

Mrs. Ashwood could not stand the dreadful twilight.

"But take away your lamp and you'll have light enough from the sunset, responded Jack.

That was just what she didn't want! The light from the window was that horrid vulgar red glow which she hated. It might be very romantic and suit lovers like Jack, but as she had some work to do, she wanted the blue shade of the lamp to correct that dreadful glare.

CHAPTER XII

JOHN MILTON had rowed back without lifting his eyes to Mrs. Ashwood's receding figure. He believed that he was right in declining her invitation, although he had a miserable feeling that it entailed seeing her for the last time. With all that he believed was his previous experience of the affections, he was still so untutored as to be confused as to his reasons for declining, or his right to have been shocked and disappointed at her manner. It seemed to him sufficiently plain that he had offended the most perfect woman he had ever known without knowing more. The feeling he had for her was none the less powerful because, in his great simplicity, it was vague and unformulated. And it was a part of this strange simplicity that in his miserable loneliness his thoughts turned unconsciously to his dead wife for sympathy and consolation. Loo would have understood him!

Mr. Fletcher, who had received him on his arrival with singular effusiveness and cordiality, had put on their final arrangements until after dinner, on account of pressing business. It was therefore with some surprise that an hour before the time he was summoned to Fletcher's room. He was still more surprised to find him sitting at his desk from which a number of business papers and letters had been hurriedly thrust aside to make way for a manuscript. A single glance at it was enough to show the unhappy John Milton that it was the one he had sent to Mrs. Ashwood. The colour flushed to his cheek and he felt a mist before his eyes. His employer's face on the contrary was quite pale, and his eyes were fixed on Harcourt with a singular intensity. His voice too, although under great control, was hard and strange.

"Read that," he said, handing the young man a letter.

The colour again streamed into John Milton's face as he recognized the hand of Mrs. Ashwood, and remained there while he read it. When he put it down, however, he raised his frank eyes to Fletcher's and said with a certain dignity and manliness: "What she says is the truth, sir. But it is I who am alone at fault. This manuscript is merely my stupid idea of a very simple story she was once kind enough to tell me when we were talking of strange occurrences in real life, which she thought I might some time make use of in my work. I tried to embellish it, and failed. That's all. I will take it back—it was written only for her."

There was such an irresistible truthfulness and sincerity in his voice and manner, that any idea of complicity with the sender was dismissed from Fletcher's mind. As Harcourt, however, extended his hand for the manuscript Fletcher interfered.

"You forget that you gave it to her, and she has sent it to me. If I don't keep it, it can be returned to her only. Now may I ask who is this lady who takes such an interest in your literary career? Have you known her long? Is she a friend of your family?"

The slight sneer that accompanied his question restored the natural colour to the young man's face but kindled his eye ominously.

"No," he said briefly, "I met her accidentally about two months ago and as accidentally found out that she had taken an interest in one of the first things I ever wrote for your paper. She neither knew you nor me. It was then that she told me this story; she did not even then know who I was, though she had met some of my family. She was very good and has generously tried to help me."

Fletcher s'eyes remained fixed upon him.

"But this tells me only what she is, not who she is."

"I am afraid you must inquire of her brother, Mr. Shipley," said Harcourt curtly.

"Shipley?"

"Yes; he is travelling with her for his health, and they are going south when the rains come. They are wealthy Philadelphians, I believe, and—and she is a widow."

Fletcher picked up her note and glanced again at the signature, "Constance Ashwood." There was a moment of silence, when he resumed in quite a different voice "It's odd I never met them nor they me."

As he seemed to be waiting for a response, John Milton said simply: "I suppose it's because they have not been here long, and are somewhat reserved."

Mr. Fletcher laid aside the manuscript and letter, and. took up his apparently suspended work.

"When you see this Mrs.—Mrs. Ashwood again, you might say—"

"I shall not see her again," interrupted John Milton, hastily.

Mr. Fletcher shrugged his shoulders. "Very well," he said with a peculiar smile, "I will write to her. Now, Mr. Harcourt," he continued with a sudden business brevity, "if you please we'll drop this affair and attend to the matter for which I just summoned you. Since yesterday an important contract for which I have been waiting is concluded, and its performance will take me East at once. I have made arrangements that you will be left in the literary charge of the Clarion. It is only a fitting recompense that the paper owes to you and your father—to whom I hope to see you presently reconciled. But we won't discuss that now! As my affairs take me back to Los Gatos within half an hour I am sorry I cannot dispense my hospitality in person,—but you will dine and sleep here to-night. Good-Bye. As you go out will you please send up Mr. Jackson to me?" He nodded briefly, seemed to plunge instantly into his papers again, and John Milton was glad to withdraw.

The shock he had felt at Mrs. Ashwood's frigid disposition of his wishes and his manuscript had benumbed him to any enjoyment or appreciation in the change of his fortune. He wandered out of the house and descended to the beach in a dazed, bewildered way, seeing only the words of her letter to Fletcher before him, and striving to grasp some other meaning from them than their coldly practical purport. Perhaps this was her cruel revenge for his telling her not to write to him. Could she not have divined it was only his fear of what she might say! And now it was all over!

She had washed her hands of him with the sending of that manuscript and letter, and he would pass out of her memory as a foolish, conceited, ingrate—perhaps a figure as wearily irritating and stupid to her as the cousin she had known. He mechanically lifted his eyes to the distant hotel: the glow was still in the western sky, but the blue lamp was already shining in the window. His cheek flushed quickly, and he turned away as if she could have seen his face. Yes—she despised him, and that was his answer!

When he returned, Mr. Fletcher had gone. He dragged through a dinner with Mr. Jackson, Fletcher's secretary, and tried to realize his good fortune in listening to the subordinate's congratulations. "But I thought," said Jackson, "you had slipped up on your luck to-day, when the old man sent for you. He was quite white and ready to rip out about something that had just come in. I suppose it was one of those anonymous things against your father—the old man's dead set against 'em now." But John Milton heard him vaguely, and presently excused himself for a row on the moonlit bay.

The active exertion, with intervals of placid drifting along the land-locked shore, somewhat soothed him. The heaving Pacific beyond was partly hidden in a low creeping fog, but the curving bay was softly radiant. The rocks whereon she sat that morning, the hotel where she was now quietly reading, were outlined in black and silver. In this dangerous contiguity it seemed to him that her presence returned—not the woman who had met him so coldly; who had penned those lines; the woman from whom he was now parting for ever, but the blameless ideal he had worshipped from the first, and which he now felt could never pass out of his life again! He recalled their long talks, their rarer rides and walks in the city; her quick appreciation and ready sympathy; her pretty curiosity and half-maternal consideration of his foolish, youthful past; even the playful way that she sometimes seemed to make herself younger as if to better understand him. Lingering at times in the shadow of the headland, he fancied he saw the delicate nervous outlines of her face near his own again; the faint shading of her brown lashes, the soft intelligence of her grey eyes. Drifting idly in the placid moonlight, pulling feverishly across the swell of the channel, or lying on his oars in the shallows of the rocks, but always following the curves of the bay, like a bird circling around a lighthouse, it was far in the night before he at last dragged his boat upon the sand. Then he turned to look once more at her distant window. He would be away in the morning and he should never see it again! It was very late, but the blue light seemed to be still burning unalterably and inflexibly.

But even as he gazed a change came over it. A shadow seemed to pass before the blind; the blue shade was lifted; for an instant he could see the colourless starlike point of the light itself show clearly. It was over now: she was putting out the lamp. Suddenly he held his breath! A roseate glow gradually suffused the window like a burning blush; the curtain was drawn aside, and the red lamp shade gleamed out surely and steadily into the darkness.

Transfigured and breathless in the moonlight, John Milton gazed on it. It seemed to him the dawn of Love !

CHAPTER XIII

THE winter rains had come. But so plenteously and persistently, and with such fateful preparation of circumstance, that the long-looked-for blessing presently became a wonder, an anxiety, and at last a slowly widening terror. Before a month had passed every mountain, stream, and watercourse, surcharged with the melted snows of the Sierras, had become a great tributary; every tributary a great river until, pouring their great volume into the engorged channels of the Americain and Sacramento rivers, they overleaped their banks, and became as one vast inland sea. Even to a country already familiar with broad and striking catastrophe, the flood was a phenomenal one. For days the sullen overflow lay in the valley of the Sacramento, enormous, silent, currentless—except where the surplus waters rolled through Carquinez Straits, San Francisco Bay, and the Golden Gate, and reappeared as the vanished Sacramento River, in an outflowing stream of fresh and, turbid water fifty miles at sea.

Across the vast inland expanse, brooded, over by a leaden sky, leaden rain fell, dimpling like shot the sluggish pools of the flood; a cloudy chaos of fallen trees, drifting barns and out-huses, waggons and agricultural implements, moved over the surface of the waters, or circled slowly around the outskirts of forests that stood ankle deep in ooze and the current "which in serried phalanx they resisted still. As night fell these forms became still more vague and chaotic, and were interspersed with the scattered lanterns and flaming torches of relief-boats, or occasionally the high terraced gleaming windows of the great steamboats feeling their way along the lost channel. At times the opening of a furnace door shot broad bars of light across the sluggish stream and into the branches of dripping and drift-encumbered trees; at times the looming smoke-stacks sent out a pent-up breath of sparks that illuminated the inky chaos for a moment, and then fell as black and dripping rain. Or perhaps a hoarse shout from some faintly outlined bulk on either side brought a quick response from the relief-boats, and. the detaching of a canoe with a blazing pine-knot in its bow into the outer darkness.

It was late in the afternoon when Lawrence Grant, from the deck of one of the larger tugs, sighted what had been once the estuary of Sidon Creek. The leader of a party of scientific observation and relief he had kept a tireless watch of eighteen hours, keenly noticing the work of devastation, the changes in the channel, the prospects of abatement, and the danger that still threatened. He had passed down the length of the submerged Sacramento valley, through the Straits of Carquinez, and was now steaming along the shores of the upper reaches of San Francisco Bay. Everywhere the same scene of desolation—vast stretches of tule land, once broken up by cultivation and dotted with dwellings, now clearly erased on that watery chart; long lines of symmetrical perspective, breaking the monotonous level, showing orchards buried in the flood; Indian mounds and natural eminences covered with cattle or hastily erected camps; half submerged houses, whose solitary chimneys, however, still gave signs of an undaunted life within; isolated groups of trees, with their lower branches heavy with the unwholesome fruit of the flood, in wisps of hay and straw, rakes and pitchforks, or pathetically sheltering some shivering and forgotten house-hold pet. But everywhere the same dull, expressionless, placid tranquillity of destruction—a horrible levelling of all things in one bland, smiling equality of surface, beneath which agony, despair, and ruin were deeply buried and forgotten: a catastrophe without convulsion—a devastation voiceless, passionless, and supine.

The boat had slowed up before what seemed to be a collection of disarranged houses with the current flowing between lines that indicated the existence of thoroughfares and streets. Many of the lighter wooden buildings were huddled together on the street corners with their gables to the flow; some appeared, as if they had fallen on their knees, and others lay complacently on their sides, like the houses of a child's toy village. An elevator still lifted itself above the other warehouses; from the centre of an enormous square pond, once the plaza, still arose a "Liberty pole," or flagstaff, which now supported a swinging lantern, and in the distance appeared the glittering dome of some public building. Grant recognized the scene at once. It was all that was left of the invincible youth of Tasajara!

As this was an objective point of the scheme of survey and relief for the district, the boat was made fast to the second story of one of the warehouses. It was now used as a general store and depôt, and bore a singular resemblance in its interior to Harcourt's grocery at Sidon. This suggestion was the more fatefully indicated by the fact that half-a-dozen men were seated around a stove in the centre, more or less given up to a kind of philosophical and lazy enjoyment of their enforced idleness. And when to this was added the more surprising coincidence that the party consisted of Billings, Peters, and Wingate,—former residents of Sidon and first citizens of Tasajara—the resemblance was complete.

They were ruined,—but they accepted their common fate with a certain Indian stoicism and Western sense of humour that for the time lifted them above the vulgar complacency of their former fortunes. There was a deep-seated, if coarse and irreverent, resignation in their philosophy. At the beginning of the calamity it had been roughly formulated by Billings in the statement that "It wasn't anybody's fault; there was nobody to kill, and what couldn't be reached by a Vigilance Committee there was no use resolootin over." When the Rev. Doctor Pilsbury had suggested an appeal to a Higher Power, Peters had replied good-humouredly, that a "Creator who could fool around with them in that style was above being interfered with by prayer." At first the calamity had been a thing to fight against; then it became a practical joke, the sting of which was lost in the victims' power of endurance and assumed ignorance of its purport. There was something almost pathetic in their attempts to understand its peculiar humour.

"How about that Europ-e-an trip o' yours, Peters?" said Billings meditatively, from the depths of his chair. "Looks as if those Crowned Heads over there would have to wait till the water goes down considerable afore you kin trot out your wife and darters before 'em!"

"Yes," said Peters, "it rather pints that way; and ez far ez I kin see Mame Billings ain't goin' to no Saratoga, neither, tins year."

"Reckon the boys won't hang about old Harcourt's Free Library to see the girls home from lectures and singing-class much this year," said Wingate. "Wonder if Harcourt ever thought o' this the day he opened it, and made that rattlin' speech o' his about the new property? Clark says everything built on that made ground has got to go after the water falls. Rough on Harcourt after all his other losses, eh? He oughter have closed up with that scientific chap, Grant, and married him to Clementina while the big boom was on—"

"Hush!" said Peters, indicating Grant, who had just entered quietly.

"Don't mind me, gentlemen, said Grant, stepping towards the group with a grave but perfectly collected face; "on the contrary, I am very anxious to hear all the news of Harcourt's family I left for New York before the rainy season, and have only just got back."

His speech and manner appeared to be so much in keeping with the prevailing grim philosophy that Billings, after a glance at the others, went on, "Ef you left afore the first rains," said he, "you must have left only the steamer ahead, of Fletcher, when he run on with Clementina Harcourt, and you might have come across them on their wedding-trip in New York."

Not a muscle of Grant's face changed under their eager and cruel scrutiny. "No, I didn't," he returned quietly. "But why did she run away? Did the father object to Fletcher? If I remember rightly he was rich and a good match."

"Yes, but I reckon the old man hadn't quite got over the Clarion abuse for all its eating humble pie and taking back its yarns of him. And maybe he might have thought the engagement rather sudden. They say that she'd only met Fletcher the day afore the engagement."

"That be d—d," said Peters, knocking the ashes out of his pipe, and startling the lazy resignation of his neighbours by taking his feet from the stove and sitting upright. "I tell ye, gentlemen, I'm sick o' this sort o' hogwash that's been ladled round to us. That gal Clementina Harcourt and that feller Fletcher had met not only once, but many times afore—yes! they were old friends if it comes to that, a matter of six years ago."

Grant's eyes were fixed eagerly on the speaker, although the others scarcely turned their heads.

"You know, gentlemen," said Peters, "I never took stock in this yer story of the drowning of Lige Curtis. Why? Well, if you wanter know—in my opinion—there never was any Lige Curtis!"

Billings lifted his head with difficulty; Wingate turned his face to the speaker.

"There never was a scrap o' paper ever found in his cabin with the name o' Lige Curtis on it; there never was any inquiry made for Lige Curtis; there never was any sorrowin' friends comin' after Lige Curtis. For why?—There never was any Lige Curtis. The man who passed himself off in Sidon under that name—was that man Fletcher. That's how he knew all about Harcourt's title; that's how he got his best holt on Harcourt. And he did it all to get Clementina Harcourt, whom the old man had refused to him in Sidon."

A grunt of incredulity passed around the circle. Such is the fate of historical innovation! Only Grant listened attentively.

"Ye ought to tell that yarn to John Milton," said Wingate ironically; "it's about in the style o' them stones he slings in the Clarion."

"He'z made a good thing outer that job. Wonder what he gets for them?" said Peters

It was Billings' time to rise, and, under the influence of some strong cynical, emotion, to even rise to his feet. Gets for 'em!— gets for 'em! I'll tell you what he gets for 'em! It beats this story o' Peters'—it beats the flood. It beats me! Ye know that boy, gentlemen; ye know how he use lie round his father's store reading flap-doodle stories and sich! Ye remember how I uster try to give him good examples and knock some sense into him? Ye remember how, after his father's good luck, he spiled all his own chances, and ran off with his father's waiter galall on account o' them flapdoodle books he read? Ye remember how he sashayed round newspaper offices in Frisco until he could write a flapdoodle story himself? Ye wanter know what he gets for 'em? I'll tell you. He got an interdiction to one of them high-toned, high-falutin' 'don't- touch- me' rich widders from Philadelfy—that's what he gets for 'em. He got her dead-set on him and his stories—that's what he gets for 'em. He got her to put him up with Fletcher in the Clarion —that's what he gets for 'em. And darn my skin!—ef what they say is true, while we hard-working men are sittin' here like drowned rats—that air John Milton, ez never did a stitch o' live work like me 'n' yere; ez never did anythin' but spin yarns about us ez did work, is now 'gittin' for 'em',—what? Guess! Why, he's gittin' the rich widder herself and half a million dollars with her! Gentlemen ! lib'ty is a good thing—but thar's some things ye gets too much lib'ty of in this county—and. That's this yer Lib'ty of THE PRESS!"

THE END

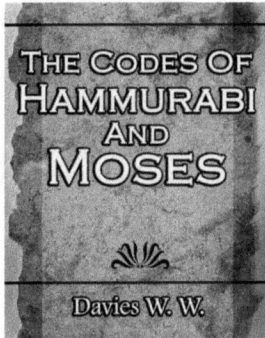

The Codes Of Hammurabi And Moses
W. W. Davies

QTY

The discovery of the Hammurabi Code is one of the greatest achievements of archaeology, and is of paramount interest, not only to the student of the Bible, but also to all those interested in ancient history...

Religion   **ISBN:** *1-59462-338-4*   **Pages:132**
MSRP $12.95

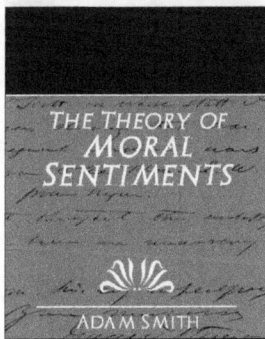

The Theory of Moral Sentiments
Adam Smith

QTY

This work from 1749. contains original theories of conscience amd moral judgment and it is the foundation for systemof morals.

Philosophy **ISBN:** *1-59462-777-0*   **Pages:536**
MSRP $19.95

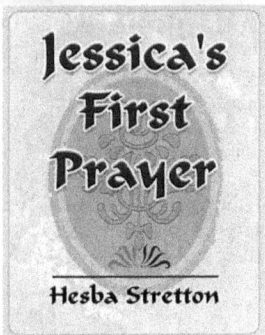

Jessica's First Prayer
Hesba Stretton

QTY

In a screened and secluded corner of one of the many railway-bridges which span the streets of London there could be seen a few years ago, from five o'clock every morning until half past eight, a tidily set-out coffee-stall, consisting of a trestle and board, upon which stood two large tin cans, with a small fire of charcoal burning under each so as to keep the coffee boiling during the early hours of the morning when the work-people were thronging into the city on their way to their daily toil...

Pages:84
Childrens   **ISBN:** *1-59462-373-2*   *MSRP $9.95*

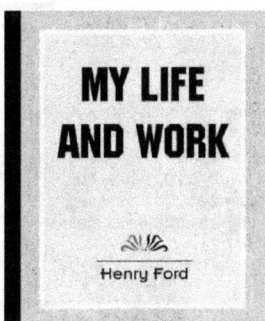

My Life and Work
Henry Ford

QTY

Henry Ford revolutionized the world with his implementation of mass production for the Model T automobile. Gain valuable business insight into his life and work with his own auto-biography... "We have only started on our development of our country we have not as yet, with all our talk of wonderful progress, done more than scratch the surface. The progress has been wonderful enough but..."

Pages:300
Biographies/   **ISBN:** *1-59462-198-5*   *MSRP $21.95*

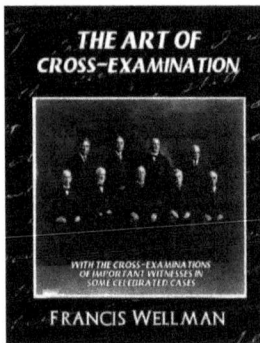

The Art of Cross-Examination
Francis Wellman

QTY

I presume it is the experience of every author, after his first book is published upon an important subject, to be almost overwhelmed with a wealth of ideas and illustrations which could readily have been included in his book, and which to his own mind, at least, seem to make a second edition inevitable. Such certainly was the case with me; and when the first edition had reached its sixth impression in five months, I rejoiced to learn that it seemed to my publishers that the book had met with a sufficiently favorable reception to justify a second and considerably enlarged edition. ..

Reference   ISBN: *1-59462-647-2*

Pages:412

MSRP $19.95

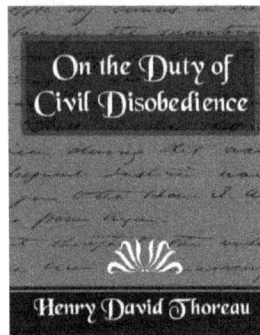

On the Duty of Civil Disobedience
Henry David Thoreau

QTY

Thoreau wrote his famous essay, On the Duty of Civil Disobedience, as a protest against an unjust but popular war and the immoral but popular institution of slave-owning. He did more than write—he declined to pay his taxes, and was hauled off to gaol in consequence. Who can say how much this refusal of his hastened the end of the war and of slavery ?

Law   ISBN: *1-59462-747-9*

Pages:48

MSRP $7.45

Dream Psychology Psychoanalysis for Beginners
Sigmund Freud

QTY

Sigmund Freud, born Sigismund Schlomo Freud (May 6, 1856 - September 23, 1939), was a Jewish-Austrian neurologist and psychiatrist who co-founded the psychoanalytic school of psychology. Freud is best known for his theories of the unconscious mind, especially involving the mechanism of repression; his redefinition of sexual desire as mobile and directed towards a wide variety of objects; and his therapeutic techniques, especially his understanding of transference in the therapeutic relationship and the presumed value of dreams as sources of insight into unconscious desires.

Psychology   ISBN: *1-59462-905-6*

Pages:196

MSRP $15.45

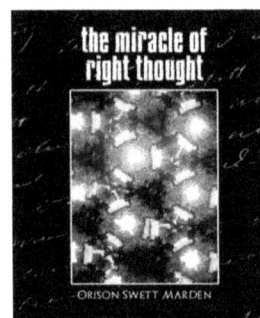

The Miracle of Right Thought
Orison Swett Marden

QTY

Believe with all of your heart that you will do what you were made to do. When the mind has once formed the habit of holding cheerful, happy, prosperous pictures, it will not be easy to form the opposite habit. It does not matter how improbable or how far away this realization may see, or how dark the prospects may be, if we visualize them as best we can, as vividly as possible, hold tenaciously to them and vigorously struggle to attain them, they will gradually become actualized, realized in the life. But a desire, a longing without endeavor, a yearning abandoned or held indifferently will vanish without realization.

Pages:360

Self Help   ISBN: *1-59462-644-8*

MSRP $25.45

QTY

The Rosicrucian Cosmo-Conception Mystic Christianity *by Max Heindel* ISBN: 1-59462-188-8 **$38.95**
The Rosicrucian Cosmo-conception is not dogmatic, neither does it appeal to any other authority than the reason of the student. It is: not controversial, but is: sent forth in the, hope that it may help to clear... New Age/Religion Pages 646

Abandonment To Divine Providence *by Jean-Pierre de Caussade* ISBN: 1-59462-228-0 **$25.95**
"The Rev. Jean Pierre de Caussade was one of the most remarkable spiritual writers of the Society of Jesus in France in the 18th Century. His death took place at Toulouse in 1751. His works have gone through many editions and have been republished... Inspirational/Religion Pages 400

Mental Chemistry *by Charles Haanel* ISBN: 1-59462-192-6 **$23.95**
Mental Chemistry allows the change of material conditions by combining and appropriately utilizing the power of the mind. Much like applied chemistry creates something new and unique out of careful combinations of chemicals the mastery of mental chemistry... New Age Pages 354

The Letters of Robert Browning and Elizabeth Barret Barrett 1845-1846 vol II ISBN: 1-59462-193-4 **$35.95**
by Robert Browning and Elizabeth Barrett Biographies Pages 596

Gleanings In Genesis (volume I) *by Arthur W. Pink* ISBN: 1-59462-130-6 **$27.45**
Appropriately has Genesis been termed "the seed plot of the Bible" for in it we have, in germ form, almost all of the great doctrines which are afterwards fully developed in the books of Scripture which follow... Religion/Inspirational Pages 420

The Master Key *by L. W. de Laurence* ISBN: 1-59462-001-6 **$30.95**
In no branch of human knowledge has there been a more lively increase of the spirit of research during the past few years than in the study of Psychology, Concentration and Mental Discipline. The requests for authentic lessons in Thought Control, Mental Discipline and... New Age/Business Pages 422

The Lesser Key Of Solomon Goetia *by L. W. de Laurence* ISBN: 1-59462-092-X **$9.95**
This translation of the first book of the "Lernegton" which is now for the first time made accessible to students of Talismanic Magic was done, after careful collation and edition, from numerous Ancient Manuscripts in Hebrew, Latin, and French... New Age/Occult Pages 92

Rubaiyat Of Omar Khayyam *by Edward Fitzgerald* ISBN: 1-59462-332-5 **$13.95**
Edward Fitzgerald, whom the world has already learned, in spite of his own efforts to remain within the shadow of anonymity, to look upon as one of the rarest poets of the century, was born at Bredfield, in Suffolk, on the 31st of March, 1809. He was the third son of John Purcell... Music Pages 172

Ancient Law *by Henry Maine* ISBN: 1-59462-128-4 **$29.95**
The chief object of the following pages is to indicate some of the earliest ideas of mankind, as they are reflected in Ancient Law, and to point out the relation of those ideas to modern thought. Religion/History Pages 452

Far-Away Stories *by William J. Locke* ISBN: 1-59462-129-2 **$19.45**
"Good wine needs no bush, but a collection of mixed vintages does. And this book is just such a collection. Some of the stories I do not want to remain buried for ever in the museum files of dead magazine-numbers an author's not unpardonable vanity..." Fiction Pages 272

Life of David Crockett *by David Crockett* ISBN: 1-59462-250-7 **$27.45**
"Colonel David Crockett was one of the most remarkable men of the times in which he lived. Born in humble life, but gifted with a strong will, an indomitable courage, and unremitting perseverance... Biographies/New Age Pages 424

Lip-Reading *by Edward Nitchie* ISBN: 1-59462-206-X **$25.95**
Edward B. Nitchie, founder of the New York School for the Hard of Hearing, now the Nitchie School of Lip-Reading, Inc, wrote "LIP-READING Principles and Practice". The development and perfecting of this meritorious work on lip-reading was an undertaking... How-to Pages 400

A Handbook of Suggestive Therapeutics, Applied Hypnotism, Psychic Science ISBN: 1-59462-214-0 **$24.95**
by Henry Munro Health/New Age/Health/Self-help Pages 376

A Doll's House: and Two Other Plays *by Henrik Ibsen* ISBN: 1-59462-112-8 **$19.95**
Henrik Ibsen created this classic when in revolutionary 1848 Rome. Introducing some striking concepts in playwriting for the realist genre, this play has been studied the world over. Fiction/Classics/Plays 308

The Light of Asia *by sir Edwin Arnold* ISBN: 1-59462-204-3 **$13.95**
In this poetic masterpiece, Edwin Arnold describes the life and teachings of Buddha. The man who was to become known as Buddha to the world was born as Prince Gautama of India but he rejected the worldly riches and abandoned the reigns of power when... Religion/History/Biographies Pages 170

The Complete Works of Guy de Maupassant *by Guy de Maupassant* ISBN: 1-59462-157-8 **$16.95**
"For days and days, nights and nights, I had dreamed of that first kiss which was to consecrate our engagement, and I knew not on what spot I should put my lips..." Fiction/Classics Pages 240

The Art of Cross-Examination *by Francis L. Wellman* ISBN: 1-59462-309-0 **$26.95**
Written by a renowned trial lawyer, Wellman imparts his experience and uses case studies to explain how to use psychology to extract desired information through questioning. How-to/Science/Reference Pages 408

Answered or Unanswered? *by Louisa Vaughan* ISBN: 1-59462-248-5 **$10.95**
Miracles of Faith in China Religion Pages 112

The Edinburgh Lectures on Mental Science (1909) *by Thomas* ISBN: 1-59462-008-3 **$11.95**
This book contains the substance of a course of lectures recently given by the writer in the Queen Street Hall, Edinburgh. Its purpose is to indicate the Natural Principles governing the relation between Mental Action and Material Conditions... New Age/Psychology Pages 148

Ayesha *by H. Rider Haggard* ISBN: 1-59462-301-5 **$24.95**
Verily and indeed it is the unexpected that happens! Probably if there was one person upon the earth from whom the Editor of this, and of a certain previous history, did not expect to hear again... Classics Pages 380

Ayala's Angel *by Anthony Trollope* ISBN: 1-59462-352-X **$29.95**
The two girls were both pretty, but Lucy who was twenty-one who supposed to be simple and comparatively unattractive, whereas Ayala was credited, as her Bombwhat romantic name might show, with poetic charm and a taste for romance, Ayala when her father died was nineteen... Fiction Pages 484

The American Commonwealth *by James Bryce* ISBN: 1-59462-286-8 **$34.45**
An interpretation of American democratic political theory. It examines political mechanics and society from the perspective of Scotsman James Bryce Politics Pages 572

Stories of the Pilgrims *by Margaret P. Pumphrey* ISBN: 1-59462-116-0 **$17.95**
This book explores pilgrims religious oppression in England as well as their escape to Holland and eventual crossing to America on the Mayflower, and their early days in New England... History Pages 268

QTY

The Fasting Cure *by Sinclair Upton*   ISBN: *1-59462-222-1*   **$13.95**
In the Cosmopolitan Magazine for May, 1910, and in the Contemporary Review (London) for April, 1910, I published an article dealing with my experiences in fasting. I have written a great many magazine articles, but never one which attracted so much attention...   *New Age/Self Help/Health Pages 164*

Hebrew Astrology *by Sepharial*   ISBN: *1-59462-308-2*   **$13.45**
In these days of advanced thinking it is a matter of common observation that we have left many of the old landmarks behind and that we are now pressing forward to greater heights and to a wider horizon than that which represented the mind-content of our progenitors...   *Astrology Pages 144*

Thought Vibration or The Law of Attraction in the Thought World   ISBN: *1-59462-127-6*   **$12.95**
by William Walker Atkinson   *Psychology/Religion Pages 144*

Optimism *by Helen Keller*   ISBN: *1-59462-108-X*   **$15.95**
Helen Keller was blind, deaf, and mute since 19 months old, yet famously learned how to overcome these handicaps, communicate with the world, and spread her lectures promoting optimism. An inspiring read for everyone...   *Biographies/Inspirational Pages 84*

Sara Crewe *by Frances Burnett*   ISBN: *1-59462-360-0*   **$9.45**
In the first place, Miss Minchin lived in London. Her home was a large, dull, tall one, in a large, dull square, where all the houses were alike, and all the sparrows were alike, and where all the door-knockers made the same heavy sound...   *Childrens/Classic Pages 88*

The Autobiography of Benjamin Franklin *by Benjamin Franklin*   ISBN: *1-59462-135-7*   **$24.95**
The Autobiography of Benjamin Franklin has probably been more extensively read than any other American historical work, and no other book of its kind has had such ups and downs of fortune. Franklin lived for many years in England, where he was agent...   *Biographies/History Pages 332*

Name	
Email	
Telephone	
Address	
City, State ZIP	

☐ **Credit Card**   ☐ **Check / Money Order**

Credit Card Number	
Expiration Date	
Signature	

Please Mail to: *Book Jungle*
PO Box 2226
Champaign, IL 61825
or Fax to: *630-214-0564*

ORDERING INFORMATION

web: *www.bookjungle.com*
email: *sales@bookjungle.com*
fax: *630-214-0564*
mail: *Book Jungle PO Box 2226 Champaign, IL 61825*
or PayPal *to sales@bookjungle.com*

Please contact us for bulk discounts

DIRECT-ORDER TERMS

**20% Discount if You Order
Two or More Books**
Free Domestic Shipping!
Accepted: Master Card, Visa,
Discover, American Express

www.ingramcontent.com/pod-product-compliance
Lightning Source LLC
Chambersburg PA
CBHW050353100426
42739CB00015BB/3378